STUDIES IN INDIAN HISTORY

BY

SURENDRANATH SEN

GYAN

Published by

Gyan Publishing House
5, Ansari Road
Daryaganj, New Delhi-110002
Phone: 011-47034999, 9811692060
E-mail: books@gyanbooks.com

Distribution Network
gyanbooks.com
India, USA, Canada, UK, Australia

ISBN: 978-93-6280-246-0 HB)
First Published, 1930

2nd Impression 2024

Printed at: Gyan Press, Delhi.

STUDIES IN INDIAN HISTORY
AUTHOR : SURENDRANATH SEN

STUDIES IN INDIAN HISTORY

STUDIES IN INDIAN HISTORY

BY

SURENDRANATH SEN

B.Litt. (Oxon.), M.A., Ph.D. (Cal.)

LECTURER IN HISTORY, CALCUTTA UNIVERSITY

In Memoriam

Narendra, Kiranendra, Amarendra

and Charubala,

my brothers and sister,

now in Heaven

PREFACE

Most of the papers included in this little volume originally appeared elsewhere. " Historical Records at Goa " and " The English Procurator at Shivaji's Court " were published in the *Calcutta Review*, " Hinduism and Muhammadan Heretics " appeared in the *Vishwa Bharati Quarterly*, " Hyder Ali's Fleet " found a place in the *Indian Historical Quarterly*, while " The Shringeri Letters of Tipu Sultan " is an elaboration of a Note first published in the *Indian Antiquary*, and " A Forgotten Maratha Admiral " is an English rendering of my Bengali article in the *Bharatvarsha*. " Portuguese Records on Hyder and Tipu " and the English translation of the " Marquis of Alorna's Instructions to his Successor " are published here for the first time. The importance of this document cannot be overemphasised. A very brief summary of this interesting paper was published in the second volume of Danvers's *Portuguese in India* and a small extract has been quoted by Pingulkar in his *History of Sawantwari State* (Marathi). But to the average student of Indian History it was, for all practical purposes, inaccessible. I need not, therefore, offer any apology for publishing here an English rendering of the first part of the " Instructions." The second and third parts are comparatively less important. I have used the late Sr. Felippe Nery Xavier's edition of the Portuguese text and the figures in crochets indicate the paging of the 3rd edition of the work. The Portuguese text is also to be found in Judice Biker's *Tratados da India*.

My thanks are due to my friend and pupil, Mr. Surathchandra Sengupta, M.A., for preparing the Index. I also beg to acknowledge my obligations to my friends Dr. P. Bragança Cunha and Mr. A. C. Ghatak, M.A. of the Calcutta University Press.

The original Portuguese spelling of Indian place and personal names has usually been retained but in some cases the more correct form has been used after once or twice indicating how the word was spelt in. Portuguese, *e.g.* Bounsulo and Bhonsla; Caruar and Karwar.

Senate House :

25th July, 1930. S. N. S.

CONTENTS

STUDIES IN INDIAN HISTORY

HISTORICAL RECORDS AT GOA

The Portuguese were the first European nation to visit India by an entirely maritime route. Vasco da Gama arrived at Calicut in 1498. He was followed by other naval leaders and diplomatic relation was soon established with the petty rulers of the South. They obtained a permanent foothold in India when Albuquerque took possession of Goa for the second time. But they did not confine their activities to commerce alone. Some of the Portuguese adventurers committed piracy in Indian waters, while others found a suitable outlet for their military ardour in the armies of native princes. It is commonly believed that the superiority of European arms and military discipline was for the first time demonstrated in India by the French, when Dupleix repulsed from the ramparts of Madras the numerous hordes of Anwaruddin, Nawab of Arcot. But long before that event Pacheco and his hundred comrades had earned an eternal fame for their country and countrymen by their gallant defence of Cochin against an army of 50,000 sent by the Zamorin. Portuguese military adventurers were thereafter welcomed by every Deccan prince. They fought for the Raja of Vijayanagar against his Muslim enemies, they entered the army of the Raja of Canara, they served in the artillery of the celebrated Bahadur Shah of Gujrat and the Portuguese pirates soon extended their sphere of activity to the Bay of Bengal. They played an important part in Indian History for more than a century and their records cannot but throw a flood of light on many of its obscure corners. It is well known that Sewel based his classical work on the History of Vijayanagar upon two Portuguese chronicles published by Prof. David Lopez of Lisbon under the title of *Chronica dos Reys de Bisnaga.* Grant Duff makes many references to Portuguese records in his immortal History of the Marathas. The India Office deputed Frederick Charles Danvers to study the Portuguese records at Lisbon and Evora and the results of his labours have been embodied in two stout volumes on the Portuguese in India. But much has yet to be done. The old kingdom of Vijayanagar and the now defunct Maratha empire were not the only Indian powers with whom the Portuguese had political and commercial dealings. Their correspondence with the kings of Bijapur, whom they call Idalxa or Idalcão, cannot be safely ignored by a student of the history of that kingdom. Nor can a historian of Mysore afford to be indifferent to the numerous letters addressed by successive Viceroys and Secretaries of State to Hyder Ali, Tipu, Hayat Saheb, Raghunath Angria, the Admiral of Hyder's fleet and others. What light the Portuguese records, when carefully and critically studied, can throw on the history of our own province has been shown by the Rev. Fr. Hosten, but I cannot pass on without quoting some extracts from one document which has hitherto received but little notice though it has been published in Judice Biker's monumental collection of treaties and peace. The original is in Portugal and not at Goa, but its importance affords ample justification for its reproduction here. It is a treaty between Paramananda, Raja of Chandradwip or Bakla and Dom Constantino de Braganza, Viceroy of India, concluded at Goa on the 30th April, 1559.

I. Treaty with the Raja of Bakla.

Very little is known about Paramananda, except that he succeeded his maternal grandfather Krishna Ballava on the throne of Kachua. Mr. Beveridge writes, " He was the son of Balabhadra Bosu, and with him commenced the Bosu family. Parmanand was succeeded by Jagadanand, who was drowned in the Ganges." It appears that the King of Bakla had sent two envoys, Nematcão and Guannu Bysuar,* to Goa. The former was undoubtedly a Muhammadan, as his name Niamat Khan † shows, the latter name has been however

* Can it be Kanu or Ganu Biswas?

† There is a village called Niamati in the District of Bakargunge.

corrupted beyond recognition, but probably he was a Hindu as he is styled in the preamble of the treaty as Veedor da fazenda de El Rei, Parmananda Ray, Rei de Bacalaa or the Dewan of Raja Parmananda, King of Bakla. The first article of the treaty provides, that His Highness the King of Bakla will open the port of Bakla or any other port in his kingdom that may be convenient, so that the ships and boats of the Portuguese, as were willing, might go there with his license in the same manner as they used to go to the great port of Bengal (Chittagong) and to other ports of that coast from Paigâo to the port of Bakla, with their goods and merchandise, not being spoils of war, and no ship of the said Portuguese nor their goods shall go to the said ports that were on the said coast from Paigâo to Bakla and also that the Capitâo mor (Chief Captain or Commodore) who used to leave for Chittagong and the Portuguese ships shall go there no more but all shall go to the said port of Bakla and any one who may do the contrary shall be punished and all persons carrying on trade there (with Chittagong) shall lose their ships and goods which will be confiscated by my master the King and they will be punished as rebels. The port, selected by the King of Bakla for the said purpose shall be such as will afford security to the ships, provided that the above-mentioned limit from Paigâo to Bakla shall not be outside the boundary of Bengal and the Chittagong coast.

The second article lays down that all Portuguese and their vessels that may go to the said port of the King of Bakla to buy or sell goods shall pay the ancient custom duties of the said port and the said duties will not be in any way raised or enhanced. According to the third article the King of Bakla made himself responsible for supplying the Portuguese ships visiting his port with all commodities and merchandise that were manufactured in the whole of the coast land from Paigâo to Bakla so that the ships might not return without the cargo that could be purchased in the country or could be procured by an agreement between the Portuguese and the merchants who bring them or the said king and his officers should they happen to possess them. The fourth article lays down that the said king shall not permit any tyranny or injustice to be committed against the Portuguese Captain-mor and merchants in his port and in his lands but he will show them all favour and give them all help that contribute to friendly relations and induce them to come there in the future.

The Portuguese in their turn were naturally willing to reciprocate and the fifth article deals with the concessions that they were to make in favour of the Bengali Raja and his subjects. The Viceroy undertook to furnish them each year with four *cartazes* (passports or naval licenses) so that four of his ships could freely navigate in different parts of the Indian Ocean. Two of these *cartazes* were for two ships going to the city of Goa where they were to pay the duties for the goods they might carry and in case they failed to come to the said city for loss of time or monsoon or on any other account they might go to any other part of Goa but they were to pay their duties for the cargo at the custom house of Goa as if they had come to that city. One ship of the Bakla Raja was permitted to go to Urmuz (Ormuz) and another to Malaqua (Molucca) but they were not to visit any port belonging to the enemies of the Portuguese. The sixth article says that in case the said king has war with other kings, lords and chieftains, the Captain-mor who may be there shall give him all necessary help with all the Portuguese against his enemies and the said Raja shall pay the expenses of all who enter his service and he will further have to guard against all loss that the Portuguese may suffer in their goods in helping him. The seventh article shows that the King of Bakla was to occupy a somewhat subordinate position to that of the King of Portugal for he was to pay an annual tribute in the said port and the tribute was to consist of the following articles :

> Five thousand candis * of good fresh rice for the provision of His Highness's store-house and fleet.
>
> One hundred candis of good and packed butter.
>
> One hundred candis of country oil packed.
>
> One hundred candis of Tar.

* The same as Marathi Khandi a measure equivalent to 20 maunds.

Fifty fardos * of good white sugar.
Fifty Scores of traquetea † cloths and fifty scores of mazaguayna ‡ cloths.

All these were to be of a quality as one merchant would accept of another and were to be delivered to the Captain-mor who might go there for them or to any other person appointed by His Highness or the Veedor da fazenda da India for this purpose, and if any of these articles were not available in the country, its value was to be paid in such commodities as might be required by the person appointed to collect it. All these articles were to be delivered on the sea coast by the King at his cost between October and November of each year so that they might be embarked and collected in the ships that might be necessary for carrying such articles. The cost of transporting them from the sea beach to the shipyard was to be borne by the Portuguese government. The eighth and last article leaves the Portuguese free to conclude similar treaties with other Rajas of the Bakla-Paigâo coast. It runs as follows :—" If some kings or chieftains of the said coast between Paigâo and Bakla want to conclude peace and friendship with His Highness (the Viceroy) and pay other tributes to the King our

* A pack, a bale or burden.

† A kind of cloth manufactured in Malabar, see Dalgado, Glossario Luso Asiatico, Vol. II, p. 386.

‡ A kind of cloth manufactured at Mazagão in Bombay, see Dalgado, Glossario, Vol. II, p. 46.

master to induce (our) ships to visit their ports, the Viceroy shall be able to make such contracts without breaking the present treaty and shall be able to divide the ships available for the voyage in two or three (squadrons) limiting at once the number that was to go to the port of Bakla by others that were to go to other ports. The Captain-mor however should go to the said port of Bakla in the same way as he used to go to the great port (Chittagong). So long as no contract is made with the above-mentioned kings and lords, the said ships and the Portuguese shall all be obliged to go to (Raja Paramananda's) port of Bakla or where the said king may ordain and the Raja shall be ever bound to pay the said tributes even if His Highness the Viceroy makes contracts with other kings. If however he pays what these others were to give then all will be reserved for his port and no (contract) shall be made with others."

The importance of this treaty cannot be over-estimated. It shows that the people of Bakargunge on that distant date carried on a maritime trade under the protection and patronage of their king. The king himself was eager to secure a monopoly of trade with the Portuguese and thus enhance his financial resources and was prepared to make many important concessions for that purpose. The Raja of Chandradwip did not probably at that date acknowledge Muhammadan supremacy or he would not be in a position to conclude a defensive treaty with a foreign power. What drove him to such a step we do not precisely know. The ambition and the war-like activities of Soliman Shah Kerany does not explain it, for he was not on the throne of Bengal when this treaty was concluded. But the rise of Sher Shah and the fall of Mahmood Shah were events that must have made profound impression on the petty Hindu Rajas of Bengal. Akbar conquered Bengal about 16 years later and Paramananda must have felt justified in taking this precaution which however ultimately proved futile.

The treaty also enables us to identify Bakla with Kachua with some amount of certainty. The prosperous city of Bakla was visited by the English traveller Ralph Fitch in 1586 or 27 years after the conclusion of this treaty. Mr. Beveridge writes, "This Bacola has entirely disappeared, and it is only a conjecture that identifies it with Kachua, the ancient seat of the Chandradwip Rajas. Fitch does not mention how he came to it from Chatigam—*i.e.*, Chittagong—nor is there any local tradition of there ever having been a town called Bacola or Bakla." But this treaty conclusively proves that there was a port known to the foreigners, if not to the natives of the District, as Bacala or Bakla. The king also took his title from the place. When the treaty was concluded the seat of the Chandradwip Rajas was at Kachua. According to the *Ain-i-Akbari* "Sarkār Bākla is upon the banks of the sea; the fort is situated among trees." Kachua, now a village of no importance, is on the banks of a fairly large river and very near the sea. So we shall not be far from the truth if we identify the lost city or port of Bakla with Kachua. The "very fair and high-builded houses" noticed by Ralph Fitch were probably all destroyed by the terrible deluge mentioned by Abul Fazl and the absence of ancient ruins in the present site need not puzzle us too much.

II. Son of the King of Busna.

Another important piece of information is supplied by Cunha Rivara in his *Catalogo Dos Manscriptos Da Bibliotheca publica Eborense* (p. 345) published in 1858. The author of a Bengali dialogue is there described as "that great Christian Cathechist who converted so many Hindus, called D. Antonio, son of the king of Busna." There was one king of Bhusnā whose name is still cherished with reverence and pride throughout Bengal. Is it possible that a son of the great Sitaram was converted to Christianity by the Portuguese Missionaries? The question certainly deserves a careful enquiry.

Enough has been said to convince any serious student of the History of Bengal that the Portuguese sources may prove invaluable to him. But it was not my main object to examine the Portuguese records from that point of view. The time at my disposal was very limited; I had to finish my work in five weeks and consequently I had to confine myself to my own subject, *viz.*, Maratha History alone. As time did not permit me to examine more than one section of the Goa archives, I confined myself, though reluctantly, to the diplomatic correspondence contained in the *Livros dos Reis Visinhos* and the following lines, I hope, will show that the work ought to be pursued further. From the time of Shivaji the Portuguese came into intimate contact with the Marathas both as friend and foe and their records show how much we have yet to learn about the eventful career of the great Maratha leader.

III. Shivaji's Treaties with the Portuguese.

"On the 30th September, 1664, Mirza Raja Jai Singh was appointed to put down Shivaji." He believed in promptness. On the 10th February, 1665, he reached Aurangabad and on the 13th of the same month he arrived at Poona (Sarkar, Shivaji, 1st ed., pp. 120-121). Raja Jai Sing wanted to accomplish his object in a single decisive campaign and the political isolation of Shivaji was a necessary preliminary of his success. He sent envoys and emissaries to all the petty chiefs in the neighbourhood. Bijapur was both cajoled and threatened and even the European merchant powers were not left alone. Negotiation was carried on with the Portuguese through Francisco de Mello and Diogo de Mello, wrongly called Francis and Dick Mile by Prof. Jadunath Sarkar * (see Biker,

* Sarkar, *Shivaji and His Times*, First Edition, p. 125, and Second Edition, p. 115. Since the publication of this paper in May, 1925, Prof. Sarkar has corrected this error

Tomo IV, p. 126). In these negotiations also the great Rajput statesman was unwilling to waste much time, for we find the Portuguese Viceroy Anotonio de Mello e Castro writing an apologetic letter to the Mirza Raja as early as the 31st March or within four weeks of his taking over charge from Maharaja Jaswant Singh.

Shivaji had in his army a number of Portuguese officers and it was evidently construed as an overt act on the part of the Portuguese Government. But Shivaji was by no means the only Indian prince to employ Portuguese and Goanese Christian officers; the Emperor of Delhi had welcomed these foreigners as artillery experts. As usual Shivaji had not stopped here, he worked with an open mind and whenever he found a useful institution whether civil or military under the neighbouring Governments, he did not hesitate to introduce in his infant kingdom something analogous. Among his eighteen karkhanas or state establishments Sabhasad mentions *Darukhana* or magazine. Prof. Sarkar has sought in vain for its prototype among the karkhanas of the Muhammadan kings of Delhi. *Darukhana* is an exact synonym of the Portuguese *Casa de Polbora*. The Portuguese were specially noted for their efficiency in artillery and it was natural that Shivaji should organise his artillery establishments on their model.

in the Third Edition of his *Shivaji* (p. 109) published in **1929.**

The Viceroy had however no difficulty in explaining away the seeming delinquency. He had no control over the Portuguese in native service and he wrote to the Rajput general emphatically denying any compliance on his part and disowning all responsibility in the matter. "These territories," the letter ran, "never gave any help or showed any favour to Shivaji. That Shivaji has some Portuguese in his service is not enough to presume my approval of it. For there are many Portuguese without my permission in the country of the Moghul king. Some (migrated) for crimes committed, others (went away) oblivious of their duty and it is not within my power to punish them. As Your Excellency knows many Portuguese will, in the same way, be found in Golconda, Canara and with Idalsha." But the Portuguese were no longer in a position to give offence to the mighty Moghul and the Viceroy addressed another letter on the same date to the Portuguese and Christian officers in the Moghul army in which an identical protest was made almost word for word.

Jai Singh compelled Shivaji to sue for peace and ultimately induced him to undertake that perilous journey to Agra. On Shivaji's return to the Deccan, the Portuguese Government were probably again approached by the Moghul diplomats and the Viceroy (João Nunes da Cunha) offered naval cooperation against the Marathas, provided the Moghul would bear the expenses, in a letter, dated 29th April, 1667 to Mirza Raja Jai Singh. (Biker,

Tomo IV, pp. 131-132.) We do not know whether this letter reached him at all, for in May of the same year he was replaced by Prince Muazzam and the Moghul prestige in the Deccan at once sank low. Moreover the Portuguese subjects were suffering from Maratha depredations and on the 5th December, 1667, a treaty of peace and amity was concluded between Shivaji and the Portuguese Viceroy. Shivaji denied all knowledge of and responsibility for the inroads made by his people and promised to release without any ransom all men, women and children carried away by his people on the 9th November, 1667, and restore all cattle and transport bullocks (boiadas) belonging to the subjects of the King of Portugal. The Portuguese Government on their part undertook to prevent Lakham Savant and his partisans from giving Shivaji any trouble from their safe shelter in the Portuguese territories and to compel them to live in the Island of Goa for effectively checking their mischiefs. Article 3 provides for freedom of commerce and articles 4 and 5 provide for amicable settlement of all differences that might arise between Shivaji and the Portuguese.

It is doubtful whether this treaty was faithfully observed by the two signatory powers, for on the 18th May, 1668, or within six months of the conclusion of the treaty, the Viceroy in a grandiloquent letter addressed to Aurangzib himself (Biker, Tomo IV, p. 134), once more offered him naval co-operation against Shivaji and we read in the preamble of the next treaty concluded on the 10th February, 1670, that Shivaji's Captains continued to be a source of trouble to their Portuguese neighbours. Shivaji had plundered Portuguese subjects and captured and detained in his ports many Portuguese vessels. The Portuguese had on their part also captured and detained ships belonging to Shivaji and his subjects. From the scanty materials at our disposal it is impossible to say who offered the first provocation and who retaliated. But probably Portuguese objection to free navigation was the real cause of this breach of peace. They insisted on their right of search and compelled every ship navigating the Arabian Sea to seek and carry their *cartaz*. As may be easily imagined this could not be tolerated by any self-respecting power and led to frequent friction. Shivaji tried to secure Portuguese alliance against his Muhammadan enemies of Delhi and Janjira. A born diplomat and judge of human character he knew that his object could best be achieved by playing upon the fears and anxieties of the Portuguese. One of the most inveterate enemies that the Portuguese then had was the Imam of Muscat. Shivaji wrote to the Viceroy that the Imam had proposed a defensive and offensive alliance with him against the Portuguese. Whether the proposal was really made or whether it was a clever hint that Shivaji could make himself doubly dangerous by co-operating with the Imam at sea we do not know. A fresh treaty was concluded. But the Portuguese were no longer in a position to defy the Emperor of Delhi or the Admiral of his fleet, nor were they inclined to concede to Shivaji the much coveted right of free navigation. Only small boats carrying food-grains, salt and other drugs of different kinds were permitted to ply from Caranja to Goa without any *cartaz* but big ships, Galvats, and other coasting vessels of any considerable dimension were denied that privilege. Shivaji's subjects, however, could obtain under the new treaty *cartaz* for any port, other than those of the enemies of the Portuguese, on payment of the customary fee and in this respect they were to be treated in the same manner as the subjects of the Moghul Emperor. Shivaji on his part was to provide shelter and provision in his ports to Portuguese ships in distress. He also undertook not to construct any fort or stone building on the Portuguese frontier unless the site was separated from the boundary line by a river. As the Portuguese were unable or unwilling to break their existing treaty and friendly relations with the Moghuls, they offered to mediate between Shivaji and his enemy the Siddi of Janjira.

IV. The Origin of Chauth.

This practically exhausts the published Portuguese sources. Of the unpublished Portuguese records in the Goa archives I am now in a position to deal with those embodied in the *Livros dos Reis Visinhos* alone. The first volume of the *Reis Visinhos* opens with a letter to Shambhaji, dated the

1st December, 1667. It is a formal letter dictated probably by the courtesy that the Maratha Prince could expect from his Portuguese neighbours. The new Viceroy informed Sambhaji of his safe arrival at Goa. It is probable that Sambhaji as heir-apparent then enjoyed some influence and power in his father's Government or the Viceroy could not go out of his way to address this short but formal letter to him. On the same date Girmaji Pandit Subedar of Bicholy was informed that Shivaji's envoy Pitambar Sinay (Shenvi) could visit Goa as often as he liked. Who was this Pitambar? It is not unlikely that we meet here for the second time the selfsame diplomat who came to Shivaji's court as an envoy from Kudal, the same Pitambar Shenvi who was contemptuously called a fish-eating Brahman by the punctilious Krishnaji Anant Sabhasad. Shivaji knew how to recognise and employ merit even when discovered in an enemy employee. A notable instance of this is furnished by the case of Baji Prabhu Deshpande who was originally in the employment of the Deshmukh of Hirdas. He had not only been appointed to a high command in Shivaji's army but it is now well-known how Baji Prabhu had sacrificed his own life to secure the safe retreat of Shivaji. It was on a delicate mission that Pitambar Shenvi was employed by Shivaji. Probably Pitambar had earned Shivaji's good opinion by his tact and ability while acting on behalf of his former master, the Desai of Kudal, and as Pitambar, an inhabitant of Kudal, was likely to have an accurate knowledge of the inner politics of his Portuguese neighbours, it was but natural that Shivaji should select him for his envoy at the Portuguese head-quarters. Like many of his caste-fellows, Pitambar probably was a good linguist (this is however a conjecture) and possessed some knowledge of the Portuguese language, a necessary equipment for his new office. Everyone cannot convert enemies into loyal friends and herein lies the greatness of Shivaji. People who once came in contact with him were at once carried away by his irresistible personal charm and magnetism.

The first service rendered by Pitambar was, as these old records tell us, the restoration of a dancing girl to liberty. She was probably attached to a temple, for both Annaji Datto and Moropant Pingle interested themselves in her cause. But it was not for this trifling end that Pitambar had been deputed to Goa. His task was as important as delicate. Shivaji demanded *Chauth* from the Portuguese on account of some villages near Daman over which a local Raja had once exercised some sort of overlordship.

According to Grant Duff, Shivaji demanded Chauth from the Portuguese for the first time in 1674 on account of Bassein. "It is not known," he says ," by what means they evaded the payment. The Mahratta histories of Shivaji's life do not state that the Portuguese ever admitted the 'Chouth' but frequent mention is made of their having paid tribute, and probably some compromise was made on this occasion." Prof. Sarkar mentions a Maratha raid against Daman in 1676 but opines that no permanent gain resulted from this campaign. Whether any permanent gain resulted from this expedition it is very difficult to say but it is almost clear that Pitambar's embassy to Goa was certainly the direct outcome of the apparently fruitless campaign. Chauth had been demanded by Shivaji and raids had been made to enforce his demand and then probably the Portuguese offered to discuss the vexed question and amicably settle it. Prof. Takkhav goes nearer the truth when he says, " The territory of this prince (the Raja of Ramnagar) comprised a few mountain forts, the outlying territories on the sea-coast forming the district of Daman, being under the Portuguese. The latter were accustomed to pay an annual tribute to the Raja to secure their immunity from his incursions. Shivaji having occupied these mountain forts turned upon the Portuguese power at Daman. The Portuguese * * sent an officer to inquire what errand Shivaji's men had come upon. They made answer, as they had been previously tutored, that they had come to enforce and confirm the annual tribute to the lord of Ramnagar. The Portuguese willingly consented ...." Let the old Portuguese records tell their own story now.

On the first of December, 1677, the Portuguese Government sent Pitambar Shenvi a free permit to visit Goa ; on the 10th of the next month (January, 1678) the Viceroy, Pedro d'Almeida, Conde de

Assumar, addressed the following letter to Shivaji, —" Pitambar Shenvi, the envoy of Your Highness, gave me a memorial on certain negotiations that * * * * some letters delivered to the Viceroy my predecessor to which he had given no reply * * for he was occupied with some business; and I immediately ordered a diligent search for them in the Secretariat and I shall try to ascertain the particulars of which they treated, so that I may confer with Your Highness. And now the said envoy has delivered to me the much esteemed letter of Your Highness, in which Your Highness expresses satisfaction at my arrival, informing me of your good news and the progress of your arms which delighted me much * * * also it deserves the excellent friendship that Your Highness had with this State and Your Highness may be certain * * * * of the continuance of the good relation that should exist between us without any failure on my part * * * * the Prince my master recommended to me. Your Highness asks me to write to the Captains of the fortresses of Bassein and Daman that they should pay to Your Highness the Chauth (?) that has always been paid to the Choutia (?) as Your Highness is now in possession of his territories. I order the said captains to inform me (that in this) * * * (?) information that till now I have regarding this negotiation, having arrived here only a few days ago; and in reply I shall write to Your Highness to send a person with authority to make a settlement with the people I nominate, after examining the terms of the contract by which the said Chauth was settled and with which it is conceded, and Your Highness shall be positive that it being clear that Your Highness is absolute * * * there should not be any doubt that what we paid to the said Choutia shall be paid to Your Highness, and as to the rest that Your Highness tells me in his letter, I observe to Your Highness that the Portuguese are better as friends than as enemies and as Your Highness is so wise he should consider these things with care that between us may be preserved and augmented our friendship and Your Highness will always find in me a faithful friend. May God illuminate the person of Your Highness in His grace. Goa, 10th January, 1678. Dom Pedro de Almeida. (Reis Visinhos, Vol. I, Fol. 2.)

On the same date two letters were addressed to Annaji Datto and Moropant Pingle. Annaji is styled as Surnivis Subedar mor das terras de Concâo and Moro Pant is addressed as Pessua e Pradano de Sivagi Raze. The letter written to Annaji unfortunately could not be deciphered, but in the epistle addressed to the Peshwa reference is made to his demand for Chauth and the answer is exactly similar to that in the letter quoted above. The Viceroy had arrived in India only recently and he was, as he himself writes, making enquiries about the justice of the Maratha claims. In the meantime Moro Pandit was requested to send a man with necessary power to confer with the Portuguese officers. About the same time (the date is obliterated) a letter was written to Girmaji Pandit, Subedar of Bicholy, in response to some complaints made by him about which the Viceroy promised to make an enquiry.

On the 15th of January, 1678, Almeida wrote a second letter to Shivaji. "I have already written to Your Highness another letter, in response to two of yours, which I delivered to Pitambar Sinay, Your Highness's envoy. And I thought (it proper) to write this letter to offer my thanks to Your Highness for the demonstration with which Your Highness welcomed my arrival which I shall reciprocate with loyal friendship, preserving for ever the (good relation) that Your Highness has with this State as Your Highness, will experience throughout the whole period of my administration as well by the special affection that I have for Your Highness, for I had already heard much of your great qualities while yet in Portugal * * * as by the great earnestness with which I was charged by the Prince my master. And as regards the business on which the above-mentioned envoy came I shall order to answer Your Highness with all possible speed as Your Highness (sees) in this letter. The above-mentioned envoy will be able to assure Your Highness of the good will that he finds in me and the expedition that I have given to the letters I ordered to be written to Moro Pandito and Anagi Pandito in reply to those of theirs and to the Captains of the fortresses of the North to inform me with all veracity about the particulars of which I asked them to make enquiry regarding the Chouth and their answer I shall send to Your Highness; and in the said letters I have ordained them to have good relations and amity with the Subedars of Your Highness and not to permit in our lands the malefactors of the Collies and Choutia so that they may not create disturbance or commit robberies in the territories of Your Highness. I expect Your Highness will also on your part ordain the said Subedars to have the same relations and good amity with the said Captains so that there may not be between us any occasion for resentment or grievance. May God illumine the person of Your Highness in His Grace. Goa, 15th January, 1678, Dom P. de Almeida (Reis Visinhos, Tomo I, Fol. 3).

The Conde de Assumar, however, did not stay in India long enough to settle this important question. He arrived at Goa on the 28th October, 1677, but left for Mozambique on the 27th January, 1678, where he died on the 22nd March of the next year. "During the absence of the Viceroy, the Government of India was administered by Dom Fr. Antonio Brandâo, the Archbishop Primate, and Antonio Paes de Sande, who had been named in the Patent of Succession, together with the Chancellor Francisco Cabral de Almada, who was now deceased." (Danvers, Portuguese in India, Vol. II, p. 366.) The next letter on this subject was signed by the second of these commissioners Antonio Paes de Sande and was addressed to Shivaji's envoy

Pitambar Shenvi. It is dated 12th July, 1768 and runs as follows :—We have received the letters that Pitambar Shenvi wrote to me and to the Archbishop Primate, in which he represented to me that he came to this city in connection with the subject of the payment of Chauth of the territories of Daman that used to be paid to the King Choutia. The Viceroy Dom Pedro d'Almeida answered him that he would send for information (on this subject) from the Captain General of the North and from that of the fortress of Daman, and when the said information came he would advise Sivaji Raze to send a person with authority to settle this business with the said Captains after examining the terms under which the said Chauth was created but the said advice had not come and the decision that was expected has been delayed. To this my answer is that the cause of this delay arose from the embarkation of the said Viceroy for Mozambique and on that account the said Captains neglected to send the information he asked of them. It was not therefore possible to inform you that this state is not tributary to any neighbouring king. As however I desire to preserve peace and amity with Sivaji I do not take any notice and pretend to be ignorant of the information that the said Captains gave me. From that information it is clear that the said Chauth had its origin in the covenant that the villagers (Varadores das Aldeas) of the district of Daman made of their own initiative with the King Choutia, without informing the past Viceroys and

Governors to avoid the loss and robbery that his subjects used to commit in those villages. From that covenant a contract has been solemnised with various conditions that were to operate between them, and I have no doubt that in conformity with them the said Chauth will be paid to Sivaji Raze as it was paid to the King Choutia, as I am told in his letters that it is in the possession of his kingdom. To settle this business Pitambar Shenvi may advise Sivaji Raze to send on his behalf a person with proper authority for I write here upon this subject, after consulting the Captain of the fortress of Daman and examining the terms under which the inhabitants of the said villages subjected them to the payment of the said Chauth. The consideration of this affair is entrusted to the judges deputed for it, so that after the said villagers are heard and the common law and known custom relating to the Chauth are considered the final decision of this business may be made with justice. Shivaji Raze may be informed of this that I on my part do not lack the desire of seeing his claim decided so that our friendship may go on increasing. Goa 12th July, 1678. Antonio Paes de Sande (Reis Visinhos, Tomo I, Fol. 12).

In the meantime the Portuguese were still enforcing their naval supremacy upon all vessels belonging to other nations but they were inclined to be lenient to Shivaji's subjects. In a letter, dated 12th March, 1678, Tanaji Ram, Havaldar of Vingurla, is informed, in reply to his letter for the restoration of a Manchua, captured and detained by the Portuguese, that the vessel was captured as it did not carry a *cartaz* but in view of the friendship and amity that existed between the Portuguese state and Shivaji Raze the vessel was ordered to be restored. Tanaji Ram was further informed that henceforth Shivaji's subjects will have nothing but friendly treatment from the Portuguese while in their territories. (Reis Visinhos, Tomo I, Fol. 4.) On the 23rd May, 1678, Pitambar Shenvi was informed in reply to a similar application for the restoration of a Parangue that he ought to know that no vessel could navigate the Indian Ocean without a *cartaz* from the Portuguese. (R. V., Tomo I, Fol. 9.)

The relations between the two powers were certainly being strained. Pitambar Shenvi was dead and it appears that no new envoy or plenipotentiary had been appointed in his place while Shivaji's people were being harassed by robbers and marauders from Portuguese territories and their patience was sorely tried by interference of the Portuguese fleet in the sea. Antonio Paes de Sande contended that he and his colleagues were doing their best to preserve the good relations hitherto prevailing between the two states, but Shivaji's Subedars thwarted their pacific attempts. The letter Sande wrote to Shivaji in this connection is certainly interesting. It runs as follows :—Received Your Highness's letter and rejoiced to find it accompanied by the excellent news of Your Highness's health and every time I shall get them the greater will be my satisfaction. In the same letter Your Highness acquaints me with the desire that the good relation and friendship that now subsist between the vassals of Your Highness and those of His Majesty the Prince my master may continue. I am not less anxious that this friendship should be preserved and should for ever increase as I have demonstrated on all occasions afforded by the Captains of Your Highness. Your Highness has written me that some malefactors from our jurisdiction go over to that of Your Highness to commit robbery and other misdeeds. My diligence to prevent this injury and the orders I have passed on the subject are well known to the Subedar of Bichely, and it cannot be * * * * that I have sanctioned it and permitted so bad a thing that is of no use but a disturbance to the State. It is a fact that at times the negligence of the Captains is the (real) cause of such excesses. For times I have often advised them to get some of these malefactors arrested so that they might be tortured to confess (and betray) their companions to be punished in an exemplary manner or to inform immediately and send a messenger to the Captain nearest our territories so that he may go in pursuit of the band of persons from these territories in order that they might be identified, etc." This letter need not be quoted in full.

Antonio Paes de Sande goes on to point out that no minister had been appointed in the place of

Pitambar Shenvi who died and it stood in the way of prompt transmission of letters. Shivaji was requested to remove this difficulty by appointing a new minister. Sande concludes this letter by explaining how difficult it was to stop all migration or immigration from and to his jurisdiction.

The next letter that Antonio Paes de Sande wrote to Shivaji dealt with the capture of some Maratha vessels by the Portuguese Armada (dated 17th November, 1678, Reis Visinhos, Tomo I, Fol. 18). These vessels according to the Portuguese version were trading with cities of Canara then at war with the Portuguese. Shivaji had evidently complained to the Goa authorities against the unfriendly conduct of their naval officers but Paes informed the Maratha King that he had been misinformed by his Captains and Subedars who were not well disposed towards the Portuguese and who were not at all inclined to continue the peace and friendly relation then subsisting between the two states. Bitterness of feeling continued to increase and the Portuguese suspected, as the next letter of Sande shows, Shivaji's ministers of secretly helping their enemies in various ways (Letter dated 11th January, 1789, Reis Visinhos, Tomo I, Fol. 24). The last letter of this series addressed to Shivaji tells us that the Maratha naval officers had in the meantime retaliated what they rightly or wrongly regarded as a hostile action by capturing in their turn some Portuguese ships. This letter, written on the 20th of March, 1679, also refers to

Shivaji's demand of Chauth from some villages under the jurisdiction of Daman and I shall quote here only the relevant portion, " Received the letter of Your Highness, delivered by Ganu Chaty (Ganesh Sheth?), on the subject of sending Your Highness the Chauth that some villages under the jurisdiction of Daman used to pay to the King Choutia as Your Highness is now in possession of those territories. Pitambar Shenvi, the envoy of Your Highness, discussed this subject in this city with the Viceroy Pedro d'Almeida and after his departure and after I had succeeded him in this Government, I solicited Your Highness as a friend to settle (this question) and to send to that end, a person on your behalf with all necessary power to treat of the form and conditions of payment. For this contribution was paid by some villages of the said Daman under certain conditions to be observed by the two parties, in which this State did not otherwise participate except giving them that permission. All these have been shown in the letter I wrote to the said envoy to be presented to Your Highness. I now remit to Your Highness a copy of that letter so that it may be seen that I have not in any way failed in the observance and preservation of peace and amity and in offering good will to Your Highness.

Things having pursued this course, Your Highness and his ministers failed on their part (in this respect) by capturing against public faith, while in peace and amity, the vessels and goods of merchants of this city who went under our banner of the Armada of the North and were assembled in the river Zamquizara (Shankheswar) in a port of a friendly Prince. I wrote to Your Highness on this subject and Your Highness gave a reply to my letter, being wrongly informed. It was a falsehood to assert that the vessels entered your port, for the truth was that the Arabs were cruising (?) in the sea where Your Highness had no jurisdiction, neither has Your Highness any jurisdiction over the Portuguese or the Arabs" (Reis Visinhos, Vol. I, Fol. 29).

In the next letter of the series, dated 8th May, 1680, addressed to Rayagi Pandito, Subedar mor de Sambagy Raze we read of Shivaji's death. The Portuguese had been preparing for a war with him. What the immediate provocation was these letters do not reveal, but it is sufficiently clear that both the parties had enough grievance against each other. When the news of Shivaji's death reached the Portuguese Government they at once suspended their hostile preparations and hastened to offer Sambhaji their condolence and assure him of their friendship (Reis Visinhos, Vol. I, Fol. 42).

These few letters show us only one side of the shield. Neither the original Marathi letters of Shivaji nor their Portuguese translation are now at Goa. A large number of records were sent from Goa to Lisbon many years ago and for all we know, these valuable documents may still be lying unheeded in some dark corners of the Record rooms of Lisbon or Evora. But one-sided as these letters necessarily are, the information yielded by them does not lack in either importance or interest. They certainly throw a sidelight on the origin of the Chauth hitherto regarded as an invention of that resourceful founder of the Maratha Empire. But it appears from the letters quoted above that the Chauth existed long before Shivaji rose to power.

According to Prof. Takkhav the Raja of Ramnagar used to receive an annual tribute from the Portuguese of Daman. Shivaji claimed this tribute after his reduction of the territories of the that Raja. In the Portuguese letters this Raja is styled as Rei Choutia because the tribute he received was Chauth or *Chouto* as the Portuguese called it. The Raja Choutia may therefore be reasonably identified with the Raja of Ramnagar. There are many letters in the first volume of Livros dos Reis Visinhos addressed to El Rei Choutia, but time did not permit me to go through them. Since I left Goa, these letters have been carefully studied by Prof. P. Pissurlencar and he informs me that the Raja Choutia was no other than the Raja of Ramnagar. The next question to be settled is when did those " villages under the jurisdiction of Daman " agree to pay the contribution called " Chouto " to the Raja of Ramnagar. I have no doubt that the exact date can be ascertained by an enquiry in the Archives of Daman, but that the arrangement was made long before

Shivaji's birth is evident. Danvers tells us that "In 1615 a treaty of peace was concluded by Gonçalo Pinto da Fonseca at Daman, between the Portuguese and King Choutia, with whom there had been some differences on account of the latter having laid claim to certain lands which were also held to belong to Portuguese territory." (Portuguese in India, Vol. II, pp. 177-178.) The arrangement which earned the Raja of Ramnagar his title of Choutia must have been concluded earlier.

Let us now see when Shivaji first began to claim Chauth from his neighbours. Both Grant Duff and Ranade agree that Chauth was for the first time claimed by Shivaji in the year 1665 when the treaty of Purandar was concluded. It is however noteworthy that Sardeshmukhi had been claimed fifteen years earlier in 1650. This claim was repeated in 1657 for the second time, but on neither of these occasions any mention of the Chauth was made. I have said elsewhere (*Administrative System of the Marathas*) that Shivaji's claim to Sardeshmukhi was based on a legal fiction, but he compelled his neighbours to pay Chauth as a price of security from plunder and for an identical reason the Portuguese subjects of Daman also had agreed to pay Chauth to the Raja of Ramnagar. In the year 1664 Shivaji had passed through the territories of the Rajas of Jawhar and Ramnagar on his way to Surat and probably on this occasion he had learnt of the Ramnagar practice of levying Chauth from their Portuguese neighbours. In

1672 Ramnagar was conquered and Chauth was demanded not only from the Portuguese but also from the people of Surat. In the first letter of Dom Pedro d'Almeida we find a corroboration of Grant Duff's statement that Chauth was demanded on account of Bassein as well. This claim was probably dropped later as no mention of it is made in the letters of Antonio Paes de Sande to Pitambar Shenvi and Shivaji where the justice of Shivaji's claims against Daman is admitted. Shivaji did not invent the Chauth, he found the practice of levying Chauth already in existence and he quickly realised that the practice could be easily extended to other hostile territories to his great financial benefit.

The Portuguese seldom addressed Shivaji and Sambhaji as Chhatrapati. They were usually styled in the Portuguese letters as Shivaji Raze and Sambhaji Raze although Shahu and even the powerless potentates of the Kolhapur branch at a subsequent period were addressed in the Portuguese letters as Xatrapaty. Annaji Datto and Moro Pant also, it should be noted, are styled as 'Surnivis' and 'Pessua' respectively, for their new designations of Sachiv and Mukhya Pradhan had evidently not yet gained any popularity among strangers.

V. How the Maratha Envoy was Received.

Pitambar Shenvi and after him Ganu Chaty or Ganesh Sheth went to Goa as Shivaji's envoy. We also read of Esaji Gambhir Rao, envoy of Sambhaji Raze. How were these envoys received by the Portuguese Governor-General and his subordinates, what formalities were observed, how many salutes, if any, were fired on the occasion of their visit, we do not know. Biker has published an extract from an interesting document under the heading "Tratamento que se dá ao Enviado do Sevagi."* But as the date of this paper is 1705, the honours and formalities mentioned therein were doubtless meant for the envoy of Shivaji the Mad, the grandson of Shivaji the Great and son of Rajaram and Tarabai. The extract runs as follows:

"On his arrival at Bicholim or Sanquelim, or Ponda or at any other place, the envoy informs the Viceroy how he is lodged there, by letters and epistles that he brings in his charge soliciting an audience. On getting this information the envoy is provided with houses with six chairs, one footstool, one side board and a skiff, he is advised as to the day he should come, assigning the place where he should come, and on the day fixed, a Manchua of the state or of the treasury, equipped with awnings of scarlet cloth and curtains of silk is sent to bring him. The Captain of the Manchua and an Adjutant go in it and lead the envoy between them to the landing place, whence word is sent to the Viceroy or Governor, and some men of high rank and

* Biker, Vol. V, pp. 12-13.

noble birth who attend the house and some Ministers attending the Viceroy come to receive him at the stairs. The envoy enters, bows thrice and delivers to the Viceroy the letter and presents he brings, which the Viceroy receives on foot below the canopy and at once hands them to the Secretary of State, who is on his right. After dismissal the envoy comes to lodge in the houses appointed for him accompanied by two mounted Adjutants, and the Factor of His Majesty sends him some refreshment of fruits to the value of sixty Xerafins. From there he solicits audience which is given without further formalities and he is always received on foot. On the day of his departure, when the envoy comes to the presence of the Viceroy, the Secretary delivers to the Viceroy the reply and the present and he gives them with his own hands to the envoy who receives them with salutes and some courteous words. If he wants to go by sea the envoy is given a ship, and two Adjutants or one accompany him according to the wish of the Viceroy ; and the same is done if he goes by land to the frontier of our territories." Only after the wars, the Conde de Alvor * received the envoy of the said Shivaji with the title of ambassador with the same treatment as is accorded to the ambassador of the King of Canara.

* Francisco de Tavora, Conde de Alvor, was Viceroy of Portuguese India from 1681 to 1686. The war mentioned is the one Sambhaji waged against him. The word Shivaji therefore stands here for Maratha kings in general.

VI. Naval activities under Sambhaji.

Conde de Alvor had to fight desperately against Sambhaji for the defence of Goa. The war, however, was of his own seeking. The Viceroy had imprudently identified himself with the Mughal cause and Sambhaji could not afford to see Goa converted into a Mughal naval base. In science, of course, the Marathas were no match for their western enemies, but Sambhaji was a better strategist than the Count of Alvor. He led his army with so much resolution that many towns in Portuguese India were captured and the safety of the metropolis was seriously threatened. It was saved only by the sudden arrival of the Mughal reinforcement, called to the scene in the nick of time, as the fervent Christians of those days believed, by the celebrated Saint Francis Xavier, to whose care the despairing Viceroy had confided the defence. The details of this war are so well known that I need not deal with them here, most of the records bearing upon the subject have been published by the celebrated Luso-Indian scholar, the late Sr. J. A. Ismael Gracias. I propose here to confine myself to the letters embodied in the second volume of *Livros dos Reis Visinhos*.

On the 28th of July, 1682, a letter was addressed to Sambhaji (R. V. Tomo II, Fol. 16) offering congratulations on the birth of a son. As Shahu was born shortly before, he was undoubtedly the prince whose birth offered the Portuguese a suitable opportunity for making friendly overtures, for in this letter the Portuguese had expressed their desire for friendship and peace. Their merchantmen were being harassed by the Maratha navy, as we read in a previous letter addressed to 'Essagi Gambir Rao,' envoy of Sambhaji, that some Galvats belonging to Portuguese subjects had been captured by Sambhaji's Subedars and Havaldars (Fol. 14). The Portuguese were quite willing to make some concessions to Sambhaji to purchase his friendship. From the time of Shivaji to the days of the Peshwas the Marathas had often to purchase powder and balls from their Portuguese neighbours and Sambhaji needed a large quantity of ammunition for his war against the Mughals. He had entrusted this business to Esaji Gambhir Rao and the Portuguese, as another letter addressed to Sambhaji on the 28th July, 1682, shows, were quite willing to give him every facility for purchase and transport of war materials he needed. The letter runs as follows:

After the envoy Esaji Gambhir Rao had delivered to me Your Highness' letter of welcome, he gave me another letter, in which Your Highness informed me that Your Highness had ordered two farms under the jurisdiction of Bicholy and Curalle to manufacture powder and purchase artillery, sulphur, saltpetre and other things ordered to be manufactured in the ports of Canara and Malabar, requesting me to direct the Captains of the Armada of this state not to obstruct those ships (carrying the munitions) and to let them and also the provision that Your Highness' subjects may take from Canara for the ports of Vingurla and Banda pass freely. As I desire to maintain friendship with Your Highness, I have given to Your Highness' envoy the necessary order to that effect, in conformity with Your Highness' request. I do not, however, experience similar treatment from Your Highness' Subedars and Ministers, who cause much harm to the subjects of this State, by capturing their ships in the Northern parts while on their way from one part of this state to another with cargo. .The ships as I have signified to Your Highness' envoy......and should order the said ships to be restored, directing your Subedars and Ministers not to commit similar outrage and violence and to behave only in such a way as (contribute to the) preservation of amity...for it can be but ill preserved, as I (have?) just shown Your Highness in all brevity, by treatment of other sort as these hostilities. May God illumine Your Highness' soul! (Fol. 16.)

On the same date a third letter was addressed to Sambhaji (Fol. 17) in which the Portuguese Government complained that a merchantman with cargo bound for the port of Cambay was captured by four or five ships, of the Maratha fleet near Chaul and the captured vessel with all its cargo was taken to the port of 'Canssou,' on the plea that the ship belonged to the merchants of Cambay, though in fact it was the property of one Rachandrassa Bagagi, Captain of the Gujrati merchants of Goa and a vassal of the Portuguese state. The Portuguese authorities pointed out that the ship and its cargo should be restored to its rightful owner in conformity with the friendship that then prevailed between the two states.

But this was by no means the last letter that the Portuguese authorities sent to Sambhaji on the 28th July, 1682. The Viceroy Francisco de Tavora had to put his signature to yet another epistle addressed to the Maratha prince. This letter shows that Sambhaji had formed an alliance with the Arabs, who at that time contended for the sovereignty of the Indian Ocean. He had made some commercial concessions in their favour and, as was alleged by the Portuguese, he shared with them some of their spoils taken from Portuguese subjects and this naturally called forth a protest from the Viceroy. But let the letter relate the obnoxious incidents. The Viceroy wrote :

" I have answered two letters of Your Highness that I received sometime ago and I am now replying one that was delivered to me a few days ago by the envoy, Esaji Gambhir Rao, in which Your Highness gives me satisfaction on.............. I complained to the envoy of the friendship Your Highness had (evinced) for the Arabs, the enemies of this state, by inviting them for your service and offering them factories in your territories and also by keeping the diamonds taken from the merchants of this city ; and yet Your Highness tells me that the information I got about......the Arabs was not correct and they had only gone to your ports to sell horses, though the information I had, convinced me to the contrary......"

The letter could not be fully deciphered, but the Portuguese Viceroy makes here a reference to the good relations that existed in the past between the Portuguese state and Sambhaji's father, Shivaji. He requests the Maratha prince to restore the diamonds to the merchants, their legitimate owners, and urges him to instruct his Subedars and Ministers not to offer any more vexation and create fresh cause of discord. A letter to the same effect was written to Nilcanta Moresoar (Nilkantha Moreshwar), ' General e Secretario de Sambagy Raze ' (Fol. 26).

These letters and expostulations were not altogether fruitless, for we find in a letter, dated 16th November, 1682 (Reis Visinhos, Tomo II, Fol. 26), a reference to a letter of Esaji Gambhir Rao, Sambhaji's envoy. The Maratha envoy informed the Portuguese that " his master had been informed of the bad proceedings of Subedar Givagi Naique and had dismissed him. In his place the old Subedar Moro Dadagi was appointed." But the Portuguese had not relied on mere epistolary expostulations. They had retaliated by capturing and detaining Maratha ships. We read in a letter addressed to Gano-Ram, Subedar de Curalle, dated 14th April, 1683 (Reis Visinhos, Tomo II, Fol. 33) that the Manchuas captured on their way from the ports of Canara would not be returned to Vingurla until ships belonging to Portuguese subjects were restored and their losses were fully compensated. But retaliatory measures had not the desired effect, as we read in a letter (dated 16th May, 1683) to Esaji Gambhir Rao, that the ships and cargo had not yet been restored. A similar letter was addressed to Ramchandra Pant on the 17th of February, 1683, prior to the angry answer given to the Subedar of Kudal, in which it was specifically stated that inspite of the friendly professions made by Sambhaji Raze, the Manchuas and Galvats captured in the North, had not been returned, and no compensation had been paid to the villages under the Portuguese jurisdiction plundered by the Marathas.

These few letters are enough to show that busy as Sambhaji was on the land, his naval officers were not altogether idle, and the period between Shivaji's death and the rise of Kanhoji Angria was not altogether a blank in the Naval History of the Marathas. On the high seas the Maratha fleet still held its own as in the days of the great Shivaji and the Portuguese maritime power had very little or no terror for the brave Maratha sailors. To a modern reader their capture and detention of inoffensive merchantmen may appear as a high-handed act of piracy. In fact the Maratha Admirals have often been called pirates by European writers of all nationalities, but as we shall see later on, they had learnt this practice from a European nation and they rightly or wrongly thought that any ship of any nationality, other than their own, formed their lawful prize unless she carried a Maratha passport.

6

VII. Rajaram.

The first few years of Rajaram were fraught with difficulties. For eight out of a reign of eleven years he was besieged by his Mughal enemies in the fort of Jinji in the Madras Presidency. His country had been wholly overrun by the Mughal cavalry and most of his hill forts had been captured and garrisoned by the Mughals. But harassed as the Marathas were in their own land their army and navy did not cease to be a source of annoyance to the Portuguese. Francisco de Tavora, Conde de Alvor, had left India in 1681 and for the next seven years there was no Viceroy, the Portuguese Estate in India was ruled by Governors and Commissioners. The next Viceroy, Dom Pedro Antonio de Noronha, Conde de Villa Verde, arrived at Goa in 1693 and was in India for the next five years. During his Viceroyalty Ramchandra Pant Amatya acted as Rajaram's representative in Maharashtra and we come across many letters addressed to Ramchandra Pant, his lieutenants and their Mughal adversaries in the third volume of the *Livros dos Reis Visinhos*. We find a reference to the depredations of the Maratha fleet in a letter addressed by the Count of Villa Verde on the 15th June, 1695 to Ganessa Ragnato (Ganesh Raghunath), the newly appointed Governor of Konkan. The Viceroy wrote :

"I am very glad to hear of the selection of Your Honour by Ramchandra Pandit for the Government of the territories of the Concan and I am very pleased to find that Your Honour evinces in his actions a desire for amity with this estate. The Portuguese always admit to their friendship all who desire it and so also will Your Honour experience. I cannot but express my great surprise that Ramchandra Pandit should pose as a friend of this estate while in all his actions he shows that this desire is not real. He allows the Galvetas of the Subedars under him, over whom he has authority, to infest our seas and make prizes of our Parangues. This makes me unable to understand whether he desires my friendship or makes war against me. And for this reason I went to Rajapore to look for the Arabs. Moreover if the Prince Raza Rama desires to be our friend, he should not permit our enemies in his ports, for he who helps our enemies does not keep peace with us. I am ready to accept the friendship of Prince Raza Rama if the actions of his captains and officers are those of true friends, but in case they lack in fidelity and the Galvetas of these thieves continue their robbery, I shall have to punish them." (Reis Visinhos, Tomo III, Fol. 24.) On the same date the Count addressed a similar letter to the head of the Maratha Government, Ramchandra Pandit, in which also he complains that while the Marathas verbally profess a desire for his friendship their actions betray a different intention.

The Count of Villa Verde had every reason to be vexed. The sea was no longer safe for Portuguese merchantmen and considerable loss was caused to their trade by English and Arab pirates. He could not therefore be indifferent to the amicable relations that then existed between the Marathas and the Arabs. Shivaji had once hinted that he could easily find a willing ally in the Arabs against his Portuguese neighbours; his sons demonstrated by their pro-Arab policy that the threat, veiled though it was, was neither empty nor impracticable. But while the Arabs could harass the Portuguese trade in the sea only, the Maratha Generals could fall upon the defenceless villages in Portuguese India and plunder them at their will. That they did so not infrequently can be shown from three letters addressed to Rayagi Shamraza (Baji Sham Rao?) at different times by the Viceroy from November, 1694 to November, 1695.

The date of the first letter is illegible (Reis Visinhos, Tomo III, Fol. 15), its language leaves no doubt, however, as to the irritation of the writer. "From letters I got sometime ago from Your Honour, Ramchandra Pandit and Santagi Gorpada, I learnt that Your Honours are my friends, for so assert all in the letters mentioned above but I find the contrary, for Your Honour entered our territories with the sole intention of committing robbery with the people of the Ghats and this action is very bad and so disgusted me that a...........order (has been sent?) to Chaul for taking the island of Undry and not to allow it any provision, and send (to arrest?) (prisoner?) all Marathas found in our territories and to go to your sea ports and burn them." (The rest of the letter is illegible. The day and month cannot be deciphered at all, but the year is 1674; as the letter on fols. 18 and 19 is dated 13th of November, this must have been written some time previously.)

The strong language and the undoubted energy of the Viceroy created an impression on the Maratha Government and the next two letters indicate a negotiation for amicable settlement. An Indian diplomat seems to have been employed by the Portuguese Government. His name was Ramchrisna Naique and one Apagi Hiro was requested in a very courteous and complimentary letter to co-operate with him on this occasion. We learn from this letter that Ramchandra Pandit himself had solicited peace and the Viceroy was quite willing to accept a compensation, as his next letter to Rayagi Shamraza, dated 15th November, 1695, shows :

From the letters that I received from Your Honour before your descent from the Ghats I understood that (you came) as a friend, but from the information I got, I find that contrary (was the case) as your men entered our territories and robbed our villagers of some cattle; I believe you will some other time return them as also the sum of three Rupees per head you exacted from the villagers. I have already sent Ramcrisna Naique to make this complaint to Your Honour and I am still in doubt whether your soldiers committed (this plunder) without Your Honour's consent. I shall, however, believe that Your Honour is in heart a friend, if

Your Honour and his men return immediately the above-mentioned money that they unjustly took and do not (in future) venture to enter our country, as such actions are not permissible among friends. As I have written to you I shall settle this matter and I hope you will also on your part try your best. Goa, 15th November, 1695. Conde de Villa Verde (Reis Visinhos, Tomo III, fol. 19).

What exactly came of this negotiation we do not know, but the Portuguese had to again complain five years later against the depredations of the Marathas both on land and in the sea. This time the letter was addressed to Parissaram Panta, (Parashram Trimbak Pratinidhi) Vallido de Rama Raze: " Received a letter from Your Honour but find in it scanty reason for the entry that the fleet made in the river Zanguizara, and I estimate the good relations that this state always had with Ramraja finding all (to the contrary), as experience has shown me, for twice during the last year (your people) entered our villages of the North and robbed and harassed the villagers. (Your) Galvetas harass our Parangues that go from this city with provision and (still) Your Honour contends that peace has in this manner been observed." The letter ends with a threat of condign punishment and hostile treatment. This letter was written on the 23rd March, 1700 (Reis Visinhos, Tomo IV, fol. 23) and on the 14th of the next month the Portuguese Government informed Sidy Iacut Can, the Abyssinian Chief of Janjira, that their military preparations were meant " to cause harm to the villages of their common enemy Sivagi and were not intended to prejudice him in any way."

The Marathas had obtained signal success against their Mughal enemies and were now in a position to defy the Portuguese with impunity. But Rajaram died in 1700, a minor was on the throne and for the next two years at least, as appears from the contemporary letters, amicable relations subsisted between the two states. On the 20th April, 1702, Bauanji Mohite (Bhavanji Mohite) Subedar of Sindedurga (Sindhudurg or Malwan, the headquarters of the Maratha navy) was not only thanked for returning a Manchua belonging to the Portuguese Government but he was assured that the Portuguese would ever reciprocate such friendly treatment. A similar message was also sent to Parashram Trimbak Pratinidhi. (Reis Visinhos, Tomo IV, fol. 62.) The Marathas, as the next letter shows, were seeking the friendship of their Portuguese neighbours and hence this uncommon courtesy and conciliatory attitude on their part.

The Viceroy, Caetano de Mello de Castro, who wrote the letter, mentioned above, was a man of resolution and energy. He arrived in India in the latter part of the year 1703 and took over charge of the Government on the 2nd October. " His administration was chiefly noted for an endeavour to consolidate and extend Portuguese power in the districts bordering upon Goa." He waged war against the Angria and the Bhonsla of Sawantwari and reduced many strongholds belonging to the latter. The King of Canara agreed to pay a tribute to the Portuguese Government and for a short while its prestige was restored (Danvers, Portuguese in India, Vol. II, pp. 375-376). His correspondent was Hindu Rao, a brother of the celebrated general Shantaji Ghorpade, who was for so many years a terror to the Mughals in the Deccan. It appears that Hindu Rao had taken the earliest opportunity of addressing a letter to the new Viceroy for the answer is dated 14th of December, 1703* (?). It runs as follows:

Received two letters that Your Honour wrote to me. I did not respond to the first immediately as I was informed that Gançça Vital (Ganesh Vithal) the courier would soon arrive at this city with the second. He came and delivered the letter which Your Honour wrote me. I understand that you wish to preserve between this state and the dominions of His Most Felicitous Chatrapaty the friendship that formerly existed and which was firmly observed when my father was Viceroy of this Estate of India. Those memories oblige me to what Your Honour so prizes and is so desirous of—preservation of good relations between us. Your Honour will experience (the same desire) on my part and you on your part will direct (your men) not to commit in these lands

* The date given in the Livros dos Reis Visinhos is 1702 but Danvers says that the Viceroy did not arrive in India before the latter part of 1703.

and these seas the least violence to the Portuguese, the subjects of the King our master, and to give them the help and shelter they may require in your ports, as a pact of amity demands, for I have also in the same manner ordered that the people of your territories should not suffer any loss in the districts of these dominions or in the sea, should they there encounter my Armadas and should be thus favoured and not maltreated. I am glad (to receive) the account that Your Honour sent me of the brilliant successes in your war that commenced with the victories of the strongholds in the neighbourhood and (I hope) the successes will well continue and the army recover the loss (of the past) as Your Honour expects. Ganeça Vital has already twice spoken to me and he is in this city of Goa and I shall favour him in everything that he may want and I verbally told him about some particulars communicated to me. The said Ganeça Vital will inform Your Honour of the falsity of all that as well as some matter that I communicated to him and which may be useful in the confirmation of the good relations which I hope will be continued. Goa. 14th December, 1702 Caetano de Mello de Castro (R. V., Tomo IV, fol. 62).

Friendly relation between the two states, however, was not destined to last long as is evident from other letters addressed to Hindu Rao and that celebrated Maratha naval leader, Kanhoji Angria.

VIII. Fresh Troubles.

On the 28th September, 1703, or exactly nine months after the friendly letter addressed to the Viceroy, the Portuguese had again to complain of Maratha depredations in the sea. By this time the great Maratha Admiral Kanhoji Angria had risen to power and he was most probably responsible for these fresh troubles. But it will be more convenient to devote a separate section to the Angrias. The Portuguese Government wrote to Hindu Rao, demanding compensation for the excesses committed at the port of Mellondim and the Isles of Candery (Maratha Khanderi, better known as Kenery). " Your Honour's letter and that of Custtaji Pantta " (Krishnaji Pant) so the letter ran, " have been delivered to me and from them I understand that you desire to continue the good relations between the Maharaza and this state. Yet you do not comply much with the high purpose of the same (desire for friendship) and give satisfaction for the excesses committed in the port of Mellondim and in the Isles of Candery, as that must be well known to Your Honour. I do not demand such satisfaction, but expect that all that has been robbed from our subjects should be restored to them without delay." (Reis Visinhos, Tomo IV, fol. 74.)

The next letter that Caetano de Mello de Castro wrote to Hindu Rao Ghorpade also refers to the troubles created by the Marathas whom he angrily calls the " thieves of Sindi Durga, Undry and Candry." " Received a letter of Your Honour that Ballagi Ram and Apagi Nillcanta delivered to me. I feel much obliged and beg to signify (my obligation). I esteem very much Your Honour's recollection of the favour and good treatment that Custagi Panta received from my predecessors when he was in the neighbourhood of this state and the same friendship will Your Honour experience though I justly complain of the robberies and insolence repeatedly committed by the thieves of Sindi Durga, Undry and Candry. The Majestic State of the North has not punished them, expecting satisfaction from Sambagi Raze, from whom I got a letter a few days ago to which I responded telling him (everything) about these (robberies) so that he might order the restitution of the spoils to the vassals of this state and prohibit the repetition of the said robberies, so that the peace and friendship between this state and the said Sambagi Raze may in this manner be preserved. As for the offer Your Honour made me, I have already inflicted sufficient punishment on Qhema Saunto (Khem Savanta)...........As regards (?) other similar thefts, although he earnestly solicited my pardon promising amendment (of his conduct) I am not prepared to forgive him, and as he is an enemy of little power, I do not require any help for his reduction. It is for this reason that I do not avail myself of the offer that Your Honour made. I shall not forget the good will underlying the said offer and all that I may do Ballagi Rama and Apagi

Nilcanta...........they will inform Your Honour so that you may concede what may be useful........... Goa, 2nd November, 1704. Caetano de Mello de Castro.'' (Reis Visinhos, Tomo IV, fol. 105.)

This letter shows that the hostile activities of the Maratha fleet did not materially affect the good relations between the two neighbouring powers. The Portuguese Government had written to Krishnaji Pant urging Hindu Rao to punish the rebel Khem Savanta (3rd October, 1703, Reis Visinhos, Tomo IV, fol. 102), and it was probably in response to this letter that Hindu Rao had offered to assist the Portuguese in a punitive expedition against the Savanta and put a stop to his piratical exploits. The Viceroy in person led an expedition against Bisholy. one of the strongholds of Khem Savanta, and the castle was captured and destroyed. But it is difficult to understand how Sambhaji Raze comes to be mentioned in this letter. In 1704. Shivaji II was still on the throne and he was not replaced by Sambhaji II, his step brother till 1712. The reins of the Maratha Government were held by the ambitious dowager queen Tarabai, the reigning prince's mother, and it does not seem probable that she should permit her step-son a formidable political rival, considering the tendencies of those times, to have any share in the administration or to carry on open correspondence with the Portuguese. Is it by a mere copyist's mistake that Sambhaji's name has been substituted for that of Shivaji? The published

Marathi records throw no light upon this question, but if a revolution had really taken place at this date it is impossible that the contemporary Marathi records and the Marathi chronicles should be absolutely silent about it. The question demands further enquiry.

It is well known that Shivaji not only employed a number of Muhammadan sailors in his navy but conferred some important naval commands on Muhammadan officers like Dariya Sarang and Daulat Khan. From the unpublished Portuguese records it appears that Muhammadans continued to hold high offices in the fleet of Shivaji II as well. Two letters were addressed to one Dauda Can (Daud Khan), (Reis Visinhos, Tomo IV, fols. 105, 107) in the first of which his designation is given as "Sarnobata da Armada" while another Muslim officer Sahida Mera (Syed Meera), by name, is styled as "Subedar." In the second letter Daud Khan is addressed as "Subedar da Armada do Sivagy." Probably the Subedar held the chief command of the fleet and the "Sarnobat" was his second in command. So far as my knowledge goes, the term "Sarnobat" is not applied to a naval officer in any Marathi document. The first letter which was written on the 2nd of November, 1705, runs as follows:

Letter of the Secretary of State to Daud Khan, Sarnobat of the Fleet and Syed Meera, Subedar.

"The letter of Your Honour that Custtagi brought has been presented to the Most Excellent

Senhor Viceroy and when the Portuguese and the mariners of the yawl arrive at this city, the said Most Excellent gentleman will be made acquainted (with the facts) not however without some comments from the robbed (persons) though Your Honour exculpates the people of Ratranguery, who urges other causes for which they will not deliver (the ship) at the request of the Portuguese and the mariners of the yacht as they left it wrecked on a coast. But this excess and other thefts that are committed on this coast the Most Excellent gentleman intends to punish and this can no longer be delayed. Your Honour has assisted our Men of War in the port of Canara in pursuance of the good relation and friendship that you have with this state and the Most Excellent gentleman gratefully acknowledges this kindness. He has ordered all our battleships to treat your Men of War in a similar fashion, helping them in all that they may need, for the Portuguese know how to show their gratitude to those who sincerely serve them as well as to punish those who being friends act as pirates whenever they can. Goa, 2nd November, 1705."

It may as well be noted here that as close neighbours the Portuguese had diplomatic relations with the Kolhapur princes till the firm establishment of the British supremacy in India reduced Shivaji's descendants to the position of feudatory princes and deprived them of their diplomatic freedom. Even in the first decade of the 19th century, as late as 1812 Shivaji Raze of Kolhapur solicited

Portuguese aid against the well known Appa Desai of Nepani, but the Portuguese prudently refused to interfere in a matter involving hostility with the Peshwa, then a subordinate ally of the English. They pointed out that compliance with the Chhatrapati's request would mean breach of existing treaty obligations with the court of Poona, which the Goa Government were unwilling to risk (Letter, dated 2nd June, 1812, Reis Visinhos, Vol. 14, fols. 102-103). It must not however be supposed that from the time of Shivaji II downwards the Kolhapur princes have always been friends with the Portuguese of Goa. Sambhaji II had frequent differences with his European neighbours, but both the states had declined in power and prestige and the results of such differences were seldom so serious as to attract outside notice.

IX. Sovereignty of the Sea, as exercised by the Portuguese and the Marathas.

We have found so many references to Maratha depredations in the sea that it may not be irrelevant to discuss their nature and extent here. In the letter addressed to Hindu Rao we have seen that the Portuguese Viceroy regarded the Maratha seamen of Sindhudurg, Henry and Kenery as pirates. The terms "pirata" and "levantado," pirate and rebel, have been frequently used by the Portuguese while writing of the Angrias. The English also regarded them as corsair chiefs. Yet from a close and dispassionate examination of the facts it appears that they were guilty of only two offences. They captured and appropriated merchantmen that sailed without their passport and they also took possession of all vessels wrecked on their coast and the cargo found in them. This practice was strongly resented by the mercantile nations of the West and they made repeated attempts severally and jointly to reduce the Angrias, but the Marathas were simply imitating the Portuguese and exercising, as they thought, in a legitimate way their right of sovereignty in the sea.

After their establishment on the Western coast of India the Portuguese became easily the greatest sea power in the Indian Ocean This ascendancy they exercised in a high-handed manner and jealously guarded. They compelled even friendly states to seek their *Cartaz* or passport before sending their ships on a voyage in the Indian Ocean or the Arabian Sea. We have already seen that in the treaty concluded with the King of Bakla it had been clearly laid down that only four ships belonging to that prince will be given Cartazes for visiting Molucca, Ormuz and Goa. The friendly nations of Europe were not treated better as we learn from the accounts left by many adventurous travellers who were lured by the vague rumours of the fabulous wealth of the gorgeous East in the sixteenth and seventeenth centuries of the Christian era. Writes William Hawkins*—" The next day, going about my affaires to the great mans brother, I met with some tenne or twelve of our men, of the better sort of them, very much frighted, telling me the heaviest newes, as I thought that ever came unto me, of the taking of the Barkes by a Portugal Frigat or two and all goods and men taken, only they escaped. * * * It was my chance the next day, to meete with a Captaine of one of the Portugal Frigats, who came about businesse sent by the Captaine Major. The businesse, as I understood, was that the Governour should send me as prisoner unto him, for that we were Hollanders. I understanding what he was, tooke occasion to speake with him of the abuses offered the King of England, and his subjects: his answer was, that these seas belonged unto the King of Portugall, and none ought to come here without his license. I told him, that the King of Englands license was as good as the King of Spaines, and he that saith the contrary, is a traytor, and a villaine, and so tel your great Captaine, that in abusing the King of England, he is a base villaine, and a traytor to his King, and that I will maintaine it with my sword, if he dare come on shore." But neither the strong protests that the good Captain made nor the 'kind' treatment he subsequently accorded to a Portuguese officer availed him much as he tells us—" before he (the

* Purchas, His Pilgrimes, Vol. III, pp. 4-5.

Portuguese officer) departed the Towne, my men and goods were sent for Goa."

The incident mentioned by Hawkins occurred in 1608. Three years later the Portuguese Admiral, a more polite man than Hawkins' acquaintance, would not allow Sir Henry Middleton to enter the port of Surat. "The six and twentieth, betweene nine and ten of clocke wee weighed, having a gale of wind which brought us into the roade of Surat, we ridde by the three Indian ships in seven fathom. A mile from us ridde seven sayle of Portugall frigats or men of Warre: there were thirteene more of them which were within the river of Surat The Portugalls long before our coming thither, had intelligence that we were in the Red Sea, and bound for this place, so that these Frigats were purposely sent to keepe us from Trade at Surat, or else-where, upon the Coast. The Captaine Major* of them is called Don Francisco de Sote Major, is entitled Captaine Major of the North, he reapeth great benefit to himselfe by giving cartasses or Pasports to all ships and Frigats, which trade upon that coast. Any ship or Frigat which hath not the same passe are confiscate or lost."†

How rigorously this rule was enforced can be guessed from what Middleton says next. "The nine and twentieth, there came a small Portugall Frigat from the Admirall of the Armada (as they terme them) wherein was one Portugall and his Boy

* Portuguese "Captain-mor."

† Purchas, His Pilgrimes, Vol. II, p. 172.

who brought me answere of my Letter sent the day before from the Captaine Major, wherein hee used some complements certifying me that he was glad to heare I belonged to a king a friend, and that he and his would be readie to doe mee service in anything he might, provided I brought a Letter or Order from the King of Spaine, or the Vice-Roy, for my trading in these parts, which if I could shew him, he would willingly obey: if otherwise, he must guard the port he had in charge, where the King his Master had his factorie."* Even the Mughal officers had not the courage to support Sir Henry Middleton against the unreasonable interference of the Portuguese.

Ceasar Fredrike also found the Portuguese claiming the sovereignty of the sea and exercising it in the abovementioned manner as early as 1563. He wrote: " Diu is situate in a little Iland in the kingdome of Cambaia, which is the greatest strength that the Portugals have in all the Indies, yet a small citie, but of great trade, because there they trade very many great ships for the straights of Mecca and Ormus with merchandise, and these ships belong to the Moores and Christians, but the Moores cannot trade neither saile into these seas without the licence of the Vice-roy of the King of Portugall, otherwise they are taken and made good prises."† Ralph Fitch seems

* *Ibid*, p. 173.

† Purchas, His Pilgrimes, Vol. X, p. 89.

to echo the Italian traveller when he writes twenty years later—" It (Diu) is but little, but well stored with Merchandise, for here they lade many great ships with divers commodities for the straight of Mecca, for Ormus, and other places, and these bee ships of the Moores and of Christians. But the Moores cannot passe, except they have a Pasport from the Portugals."*

It is needless to quote more witnesses, sufficient evidence has been produced as to the Portuguese naval policy and how it was enforced against Asiatic and European nations in the sixteenth and seventeenth centuries. We will now turn to published and unpublished Portuguese records on the subject and find out how far the Marathas trod in the footsteps of their Portuguese neighbours and to what extent their conduct could be held as piratical. It is needless to point out that they should be judged bv the standard of the seventeenth and not of the twentieth or nineteenth century.

We have seen previously how Shivaji had tried in vain to secure what may be termed the freedom of the sea, for although the Portuguese made some minor concessions in favour of coasting vessels and river crafts they were determined not to permit any big ship or sea-going vessel to sail without their Cartaz. If the concession was not made in favour of the Marathas neither was it made in favour of their Muhammadan enemies the Siddis of Janjira.

* *Ibid*, p. 169.

In a letter addressed to Sidy Iacat Can, on the 3rd of April, 1700 (Reis Visinhos, Tomo IV, fol. 28), we find reference to the capture and detention of a vessel belonging either to the Siddi or to one of his subjects. The Portuguese Government protested that it was captured on legitimate grounds, *viz.*, failure to carry their Cartaz, but the ship was restored to its owner in consideration of the friendship then subsisting between the Portuguese and the Mughal. The letter concluded with a significant sentence that reminded the Siddi that the Portuguese were " the sovereigns of the seas and not pirates." Another letter on a similar subject was again addressed to " Sidy Acut Can, General da Armada del Rey Mogor, on the 16th December, 1715, which runs as follows : Received a letter of Your Lordship in which you request (the restoration of a) boat captured by one of the frigates of this state at Calicut and I am much surprised at the special reasons for which Your Lordship is not offended in this matter with as much sincerity as it deserves :

First of all there is no prince in Asia who does not know that the Most High and Mighty King of Portugal is sovereign of the Seas of India and the same is acknowledged by His Majesty the King of the Mughals and the Magnificent Monarch of Persia inasmuch as their vessels take Cartazes and observe all that they are ordained to do thereby." (Reis Visinhos, Tomo VII, fols. 26 and 27.)

Let us now see on what terms these Cartazes were granted and to what obligations the grantee was subjected. A number of typical Cartazes has been published by Judice Biker, in the fourth volume of his collection.* These will serve our purpose quite well, but the large masses of unpublished Cartazes still available in the Archives of Goa may yield information of no little value or interest.

On the 9th August of 1613, a Cartaz was issued in favour of El Rey Idalxã or Adil Shah, the Muhammadan Sultan of Bijapur. It runs as follows: I Dom Jeronimo d' Azevedo cause it to be known to all who may see it that in consideration of the ancient amity that El Rey Idalxã has with this state and as by the terms of the treaty he has concluded (with us) license and safeguard are granted to him to enable six of his ships to visit Mecca, Ormuz and other places, I have great pleasure in giving the present license and safeguard at the prayer of his ambassador to his ship Mamody (Muhammadi) by name, that carries four thousand khandis (of goods), of which the Nacodā† is Melique Ambar aged thirty years and has for her defence twelve swivels of iron, twenty muskets and many moorish weapons that go in it, so that she may start from the port of Dabul where she is during the present monsoon for Juda and return to (Dabul) without taking or bringing any prohibited goods, to wit Greeks, Turcs, Abyssinians, cinnamon of Ceylon, lead, tin, brass, timber,‡

* Biker, Vol. IV, pp. 181-188.

† Nacoda—Captain of a Merchantman.

‡ Madeira, and the original for wood in the above is Mato.

planks, saltpetre, sulphur, bamboo* and other things prohibited by the Government. Neither will she (be permitted to) carry Portuguese nor bring horses without any license and she will be (allowed to) bring slaves, male and female of her nationality only. (But) if there is any suspicion or information that some of these (slaves) are Christians or children of Christians, there will be an open enquiry about them in the Provincial Council, even if such children are not baptised and before the said ship leaves the port of Dabul, she will be inspected and searched by the Feitor of His Majesty who is there and she will take his certificate on the back of this Cartaz. On these conditions, her voyage both outward and homeward will be without any impediment from the Captain-mors of the Armadas of this state or any other Captain or persons, and all who are hereby enjoined will fulfil and observe these terms without any question. This shall be sealed with the signet of the royal arms of the crown of Portugal. Belchoir da Silva drew it at Goa on the 9th of August, 1613, and I Secretary, Affonso Rodrigues Guevara caused it to be written. Viso Rey (Dom Jeronymo de Azevedo). It must not be supposed that a friendly prince could get such Cartazes for the mere asking. Another Cartaz was issued only three days previously in favour of the Sultan of Bijapur who wanted to send from the same port of

* The original has bambus machos, the last word means any piece of timber, iron, etc., that is to be fitted into another.

Dabul one of his ships *Abdul Hadi* to Tennassarim (Tenasserim). The request of the Bijapur ambassador was complied with, but it was clearly stated in the Cartaz that "this was a new request not hitherto made or conceded," and "license was given for this occasion only" in order to please the Sultan and in consideration of the amity that existed between the two states.

The terms of the Cartaz granted to the King of Canara a year later were certainly more stringent. It is as follows:

I Vasco Fernandes Cezar de Menezes, (member) of His Majesty's Council of State, Viceroy and Captain General of India, etc., make it known to all who may see it that as the King of Canara has sent for a Cartaz to enable one of his boats to navigate, I do him the favour for this occasion only of granting license and safeguard. As his said ship Parmesuary by name, studded with nails, having a capacity of six hundred khandis of Goa and having for her Nacodā Hanṡamma Bapa, Currane* Pundallica, Pilot Mahama Dagi, Condestavel† Salu, Sarangue Ismal, Tandel‡ Abdul, and other persons for her navigation, carrying for her defence twenty-five pieces of artillery, thirty muskets, thirty swords, fifty lances, five anchors, the necessary (quantity of) powder and ball besides other munitions of war,

* The same as Bengali korāni or ship's clerk.

† Constable, probably a petty supervising officer.

‡ Marathi tandel and Indo-English tindal, a boatswain.

to enable her during the monsoon of the month of March or April of the present year 1714 to make her voyage from the port of Mangalor to the ports of Congo * and Ormuz. She will not carry slaves or Christian slaves or Christian children and if we have suspicion or information that such (persons) are on board, an open enquiry will be made in the Provincial Council even if such children are not baptised. Nor will she take or bring Abyssinians, Greeks or Arabs belonging to the territories owing allegiance to the Imam of Muscat. Neither shall she take a cargo of iron, steel, sulphur, timber, bamboos-machos for trade nor goods belonging to Arabs even if they are not prohibited, nor shall she take any Portuguese nor shall she go to any port that acknowledges the authority of the Imam of Muscat or that of the Angria or of any other prince or rebel with whom this state may be in war. Though it is (generally) prohibited this ship will bring horses as a special favour conceded to the said King that his ship may bring them from the ports of Congo and Ormuz. On her arrival at that port she will unload the goods she carries in that Factory and Custom house and pay there the usual duties for which she will take from our Factor a receipt on the back of the Cartaz with a declaration as to the horses she took in those ports so that there may not be any doubt that they were embarked there and not in other ports or in ports belonging to the Imam of

* A port in Persia.

Muscat. If she does anything contrary (to this) or goes to the prohibited ports and takes or brings forbidden goods, this Cartaz will not be valid and the ship shall be seized and forfeited to the *Fazenda real*. I thus notify the Generals and Captain-mors of the Armadas of this state, other Captains, officers and persons concerned to fulfil and observe these conditions in this manner and allow the ship to make her outward and return voyage without any impediment. After the lapse of a year this Cartaz will not be in force. It will be sealed with the seal of the royal arms of the Crown of Portugal and it is declared that this is the seventh Cartaz issued this summer for which no fee will be paid in accordance with one of the articles of a treaty concluded with the King of Canara. Gregorio Mascarenhas drew it at Goa on the first of March 1714 and I, Secretary Joao Rodrigues Machado, caused it to be written. Vasco Fernandes Cezar de Menezes. By the decree of the Most Excellent Senhor Viceroy and Captain-General of India dated the 27th February of 1714.

The royal personages, seeking Cartazes generally according to treaty rights and occasionally as a matter of courtesy, were doubtless leniently and courteously treated, but from the two Cartazes quoted above it is clear that even these ships could be confiscated and appropriated by the Portuguese Government if they were detected in any offence mentioned in the Cartaz. Let us now examine a Cartaz granted to a private merchant and for this purpose we give below the text of one granted to one

Govindadas Nana, a Gujrati merchant, and published by Biker.

The Governors of India,* etc., make it known to all who may see this Cartaz that as Govindadas Nana a Gujrati by nation, merchant and an inhabitant of Thana in the territories of the North, owner of a Gurab or Pal called *Savay*, of the capacity of one hundred and fifty khandis of Surat has solicited Cartaz for the same vessel we do him the honour and favour, for this occasion only, of granting license and safeguard to the said Gurab or Pal called *Savay* of the capacity of one hundred and fifty khandis of Surat having for her ballast six anchors big and small, one Sarangue Abdul Raiman by name, one Tandel called Ballu, one Gujrati Carane and two Muhammadan pilots, and for her defence nine pieces of artillery, eleven sepoys with their Caitocas † and Catanas ‡ and the necessary (quantity of) powder and ball, to enable her to sail in the following summer to some ports of the friends of

* The Government of Portuguese India was at this time vested in a commission consisting of following members: Dom Antonio Taveirada Neiva Brum da Silveira, Archbishop; Joao Baptista Vaz Pereira, Chancellor of the State; Dom Joao José de Mello, Controller General of the Exchequer. This commission was in charge of the Government from 1765 to 1768 and for the next seven years Dom Joao Jose de Mello acted as sole Governor.

† A kind of musket used by the Marathas and manufactured in India.

‡ A kind of long and big sword.

this state. She will not go to a port belonging to princes and rebels with whom this state may be in war and she shall not either take or bring on her board Turks, Abyssinians and Greeks nor carry a cargo of iron, steel, sulphur, copper, timber, bamboos-machos, nor will she take any Portuguese nor bring horses without our permission. She is permitted to carry slaves male or female of her own nation only and if there is any suspicion or doubt that any of the slaves (on board) is a Christian, or son of a Christian, an open enquiry about it will be made in the Provincial Council, even if the children have not been baptised. If anything is done to the contrary, this Cartaz will not be valid and if she goes to prohibited ports or bring prohibited goods or being of the tonnage (mentioned) the vessel carries more than hundred and fifty khandis of Surat it will be confiscated to the Fazenda real. He paid for the duties of entry and parting thirty xerafins * at the rate of twenty xerafins per hundred khandis of cargo not of commodities. Notice is given to this effect to the Generals and Captain-mors and other Captains and persons concerned that they should observe and fulfil these terms and let the same vessel make its outward and return voyage. At the expiry of a

* An ancient coin current in Portuguese India. The Portuguese Zerafin was originally a gold and afterwards a silver coin. It was worth 300 reis (pies) or annas 9 only; the word is probably derived from Persian Ashrafi, see Dalgado, Glossario Luso Asiatico. Biker, Vol. IV, pp. 185 and 186.

year this Cartaz will not be in force. This is the first (Cartaz) issued for the next summer. It will be sealed with the seal of the royal arms of the Crown of Portugal. Mathias Phellipe Rebeiro drew it at Goa on the 15th of July 1766. The Secretary Henrique José de Mandanha Benevides Cirne caused it to be written.—Arch Bishop Primate—Joao Baptista Vaz Pereira—D. Joao José de Mello.

By virtue of the decree of the most Excellent Governors of India, dated the 11th July, 1766.

As Govinda Das Nana was a resident of Thana he was a Maratha subject. We come across in Biker's collection a similar Cartaz issued in favour of one Bapugy Gopal of Rajapur under the Government of Poona. His boat was a very small one as it paid only 4 xerafins and its capacity was therefore twenty khandis only. This boat therefore could not afford to employ a number of sepoys and carry for its defence a number of artillery and a quantity of munition as did the *Saray* of Govinda Das Nana. But from a blank form of Cartaz published in the pages of Biker * it appears that merchantmen were generally well armed and well prepared for an encounter with hostile powers or pirates in an age when the peace of the high seas was by no means secure.

It is clear from these Cartazes as well as from contemporary letters and travellers' accounts already quoted that the Portuguese insisted that even friend-

* Biker, Tomo IV, pp. 185 and 186.

ly potentates and their subjects should take their Cartaz before they permitted any of their ships to sail even when the port of their destination and the port from which they originally started were outside Portuguese territories. While the friendly powers were entitled to a certain number of Cartazes according to the terms of the treaties they had concluded with the Portuguese, their subjects like Govinda Das Nana and Bapugy Gopal had to pay a fee of 20 Xerafins per hundred Khandis of their cargo for the Cartaz and if they omitted to provide themselves with such license and safeguard before venturing out on the high sea, their ship and its cargo could be captured and confiscated by the Portuguese fleet even though their mission might not have been anything but peaceful trade. No doubt on the representation of the Government of their respective country the ship and the goods so confiscated might be as a matter of favour restored to their owners, but the Portuguese, as we have seen in a letter addressed to Siddi Yacut Khan, did not regard such confiscation as an act of piracy, it was to them nothing but a legitimate expression of the sovereignty they claimed to exercise in the Indian Ocean. It is needless to say that the terms laid down in the Cartazes quoted above were considered vexatious by other nations and it is only their weakness that compelled them to seek their Cartaz and thereby acknowledge their sovereign claims.

The Marathi word Armar is certainly derived from Portuguese Armada and it is quite likely that the Marathas imitated the Portuguese in their naval practice. The Angrias as the hereditary heads of the Maratha fleet also claimed sovereignty of the sea and they could also retort like the Portuguese that they were sovereigns of the sea and not pirates. They knew in what particular manner the Portuguese, the first European nation to establish their supremacy in the Indian Ocean, exercised their sovereignty and they also demanded that other powers should seek their Cartaz after paying a stipulated fee while sailing in the sea over which they claimed to have established their jurisdiction. After the reduction of the Angria's power the same right was claimed and exercised by the Peshwa's Subedar of the Armar or Admiral of the fleet. Although Marathi records do not throw much light on the subject, the correspondence that passed between Gangadhar Pant Subedar of Gheria or Vijayadurg, the Maratha naval headquarter, and the Portuguese Government in February, 1791, leaves no doubt as to the real nature of the Maratha claim and its origin.

The Governor of Goa in a letter, dated 17th February, 1791, complained to the Subedar of Gheria that Maratha Captains had captured without cause some Merchantmen belonging to Portuguese territories. The same complaint was repeated in a letter of the Secretary of State to Bahiropant Mehendale (Biker, Vol. IX, pp. 185-186) in the following way:

" The vessels of the Sarkar took in the port of Angediva, a loaded Merchantman belonging to a merchant of that place and at Chapora they robbed the canoes of the fishermen without leaving even their small sails, besides other incidents to which I do not refer, for it seems that some of them and other hostilities which I do not mention here, might have been committed by the Bhonsla, Melondim and the Angria of Colaba who use the banner of the Most Felicitous (Peshwa)."

In reply to the above complaint Gangadhar Pant wrote to the Governor of Goa on the 21st February, 1791 (Biker, Vol. IX, p. 187) as follows: "The said vessel was in the sea and it got no Cartaz nor had it a passport nor the banner of Your Excellency. It was, therefore, justly captured, nor does it seem to belong to the dominions of Your Excellency and I am much surprised that under these circumstances Your Excellency wrote about the release of this ship." It is significant that the Maratha officer lays emphasis on the absence of Cartaz and passport in this case. We learn from the published documents of the Peshwas' Daftar that it was one of the duties of the Admiral of the fleet to grant passports to merchantmen sailing within his jurisdiction. Moreover, we should not forget that the merchantships in those days were not unarmed and when they omitted to procure the passport of a power claiming sovereignty over a particular part of the sea, their act could be construed as a deliberate defiance. Merchantships belonging to European trading companies often put up a stiff fight before surrendering to the Marathas and considering the practices of the time that permitted even vessels of the East India Company to rob ships belonging to other nations, the Marathas should not be condemned as pirates. They had the example of the Portuguese before them and they thought that they were quite within their rights when they took possession of a merchantman that did not carry their Cartaz and further aggravated its offence by opening fire when challenged.

This conclusion is further confirmed by an unpublished letter addressed to Raghuji Angria of Colaba, on the 2nd of May, 1782. The document (Reis Visinhos, Tomo 11) is sadly mutilated and some words in it has been so thoroughly obliterated that it is impossible to decipher them and reconstruct all the sentences. Fortunately however the most interesting portion has been preserved. A negotiation was going on between the Goa Government and the Chief of Colaba for the conclusion of a treaty of alliance and Raghunath Angria had suggested some modifications in the terms proposed. What his suggestion was can be inferred from the reply he got which runs as follows:

" While (you suggest) for the preservation of unity and amity, that with the exception of His Majesty's ships belonging to Goa, Diu and Daman, all vessels of the merchants shall take the Cartaz of the Magnificent Ally (Angria) and the ships of your merchants shall take mine. I am unable to accept this article and it is impracticable, for the Crown of Portugal has the sovereignty and the dominion of the Sea of Asia by first occupation and conquest, by possession and immemorial custom, and we cannot compel the subjects of the Majestic State to take the Cartazes of any other potentate."

But in the closing years of the 18th century the sovereignty of the sea had passed into other hands however tenaciously the Portuguese might cling to a point of prestige and although they deemed it humiliating on their part to seek Cartazes from an Indian prince they were not unwilling to waive the rights of sovereignty they had hitherto so rigorously enforced. The Governor and Captain-General * therefore wrote:

I desire to preserve amity with the Magnificent friend on terms that will not be much onerous to either party. I shall not do anything to your merchants even if they do not possess my Cartaz. In the same manner the fleet and the ships of the Magnificent Ally should not interfere with the merchants of the Majestic State even if they do not possess the Cartaz of the Magnificent Ally.

So by common consent the omission to take a Cartaz from the dominant sea power was regarded as an offence punishable with confiscation and forfeiture of the offending ship. The Angrias were denounced as pirates and rebels by the Portuguese and other European nations on no graver ground than the enforcement of this sovereign right in the high seas. The practice, to quote the Portuguese Governor and

* Dom Frederico Guilherme de Souza, Governor and Captain General from 1779 to 1786.

Captain-General, had the sanction of "immemorial custom."

In this connection it will not be irrelevant to take notice of another common naval practice of the Marathas. They claimed the possession of ships wrecked on their coast with whatever cargo they might carry. The English obtained an exemption in favour of their own ships and those of the Bombay merchants by peaceful negotiations, but against others this right was very rigorously exercised by the Maratha Admiral of the Fleet. In the 11th volume of *Livros dos Reis Visinhos* we find a protracted correspondence between the Portuguese Governor and the Maratha Admiral about the restoration of a wrecked Manchua which the Marathas had appropriated to their own use.

On the 10th of June, 1780, Dom Frederico Guilherme de Souza wrote to 'Dulopo' (Anand Rao Dhulap) "I solicited a sanad for the wrecked Manchua of the state which was conducted to that port.* I am sending it (the sanad) enclosed (herewith) for Your Honour so that Your Honour may promptly restore (?) the said Manchua" (Reis Visinhos, Tomo 11, Fol. 4).

This Sanad had not however the desired effect for it appears from a letter addressed to Ananda Rao on the 4th February, 1782 (R. V., Tomo 11, Fol. 135) that the Manchua had not yet been restored.

* The document is damaged and I am therefore unable to say which port exactly is meant.

In the meantime one Fokru Serang was driven by some adverse circumstances to take shelter in Goa with five Galvats of Gheria. This offered the Portuguese an excellent opportunity for retaliating if they had been so disposed, but the Serang was very kindly treated and supplied with everything he needed. This news was communicated to Ananda Rao in the above-mentioned letter and we learn from a letter addressed to Madhav Rao Narayan (Fols. 138-139) that the Serang was permitted to depart peacefully with the squadron under his charge on the 8th of February, 1782. This made a good impression on Ananda Rao and the wrecked Manchua was probably restored ; for in a mutilated letter addressed to Narana Sinay, the Portuguese envoy at the Poona Court, on the 3rd June, 1782, occurs the following : "Ia vos ordeney que pella rest......chua naufragada que fez." It is not difficult to guess that we find here a reference to the restoration of the wrecked Manchua.

We should not forget that the Marathas did not hesitate to restore ships belonging to a friendly nation, if captured under a misconception or under doubtful circumstances. The Portuguese Government of their own initiative sometimes wrote to the Maratha officers for extending their protection to Portuguese subjects and their ships in Maratha waters. One such letter was addressed to the Sarsubedar of Bassein on the 31st March, 1783, requesting him to give his protection to a Pal belonging to a vassal of the King of Portugal. (Reis Visinhos, Tomo 12, Fol. 39.) From letters addressed to Ananda Rao Dhulap and Naraen Sinay on the 7th of June, 1781, we learn that five Maratha Galvats belonging to the fleet of Gheria had robbed certain Parangues belonging to merchants of Portuguese India and the total loss sustained by them on this occasion amounted to Rs. 1,17,80,000. (Reis Visinhos, Tomo 11.) On the 16th August, 1781, or only two months later Narayen Sinay was informed that a Shibar captured on the above occasion had been restored to its owner with a money compensation for the lost cargo. From this letter it is apparent that the matter had been amicably settled.

The Portuguese documents present to our view only one side of the shield. We hear complaints of one party alone, we do not know what justification the other party could offer. Still we occasionally come across cases of restoration of captured ships and payment of compensation for lost cargo. It will be, therefore, rash to condemn famous Maratha naval leaders like Kanhoji Angria and his sons without carefully examining the naval customs and usages of the time. The European merchant nations had no reason to admire their prowess, for their trade suffered heavily and the sea had been rendered insecure for their ships by the Angria's fleet. But whenever they condescended to open negotiations with him they consciously or unconsciously recognised his authority. Like other Maratha feudal chiefs Kanhoji Angria also derived his authority from the supreme head of the Maratha empire. The Portuguese styled him as a pirate and rebel in their letters to the Siddi and other Mughal officers, but whenever they wrote to him or to his sons courtesy demanded that he should be addressed as Grandioso Amigo or Grandioso Canogi Angria. After treaties and alliances had been concluded between the Portuguese of Goa and the Angrias of Colaba, the former willingly or unwillingly conceded a status of equality to the latter and it was illogical thereafter to regard their new ally as a mere pirate, particularly when his naval practices were in complete conformity with the usages established by the Portuguese themselves. Now that we have some idea of the principle underlying the apparently piratical activities of the Angrias and the true character of their power, let us see what light the Portuguese records throw on the history of the rise, decline and fall of this powerful family.

X. The Angrias.

"The Angrias," wrote the Marquis of Alorna in his excellent report, "are the scourge of this coast from the point of Diu to Calicut. They came into prominence a little before the administration of Senhor Viceroy Caetano de Mello de Castro." The original surname of the family was Sankapal as the Kaifiyat Yadi account informs us, but nothing is known about Kanhoji's ancestors except that his father had served in Shivaji's Fleet. Downing says that Kanhoji's father was, according to one account, "an Arabian *Cofferey*, one that renounced *the Mehometan faith.*" "Other accounts say, that he was born a *Kenerey*, by a Portuguese *Cofferey* and a *Kenerey* woman, on the Island of Bombay." It is hardly necessary to enter into an examination of the reliability of these stories. Suffice it to say that Kanhoji like his father took to the sea and rose from one command to another until his daring and ability secured for him the chief command of the Maratha fleet during the reign of Rajaram. Those stirring times offered excellent opportunities to ambitious men for proving their mettle and rapidly rising to prominence.

In the first letter addressed to him by the Portuguese Government, which we find in the *Livros dos Reis Visinhos*, Kanhoji is called Canoji Ango Rao (Reis Visinhos, Tomo IV, Fol. 72). Mr. Sardesai is of opinion that the new surname of the family was derived from their old village Angarvadi. In this letter, however, for reasons unknown to us, Kanhoji's designations are entirely omitted. In the next letter he is styled "Subedar da Armada do Sivaji." The Marathas, as we have already seen, were on friendly terms with the Portuguese during the early years of Shivaji II's reign and the letter addressed to Kanhoji Angria, on the 8th November, 1703, by the Viceroy Caetano de Mello de Castro also testifies to their amity. "The letters of Your Honour have been delivered to me and I am glad to recognise the good wish with which you desire to favour (me) in everything. I did not approve of the Balandra (?) for reasons I have already mentioned and on the same grounds I did not permit its sale to the merchants of this city, but wishing that Your Honour should get this profit, I have given you license for its purchase by the merchants of Chaul(?). As that port is closed to foreign nations, I expect that Your Honour will view with pleasure the great favour I have done you and I have also instructed to give all help and assistance to the people who came in the Balandra." The letter also mentions some presents that the Viceroy proposed to send and an arrangement for the sale of some commodities which the Viceroy has asked the Veedore da Fazenda to make.

But the good relations between the Angria and the Portuguese could not be expected to last long particularly as the former wanted to establish his authority over the Arabian Sea. In 1713 we are informed by Sr. G. Saldanha (*Resumo da Historia de Goa*, Bastorá, 1898, p. 179) that Kanhoji seized a port in the neighbourhood of Chaul and the Portuguese Government, unwilling to have such a formidable rival in such close proximity of one of their important naval stations, did their best to oust him from this new post, but all their attempts proved futile.

The Portuguese accused the Siddi of Janjira of criminal indifference to the depredations of the Angria. In a letter addressed to one Dom Diogo Menedes (in the army of the Moghul Emperor) on the 15th of May, 1715, the Viceroy complains of "the treaty that the Siddi had concluded with the Angria, the pirate who oppresses the subjects of the Mughal king by his repeated robberies and totally ruins the port of Surat. If the Siddi had made some movements by land last year, when I besieged the Angria by sea at Colaba, it is certain that this rebel would have been annihilated." (Ismael Gracias, *Uma Dona Portuguesa no Corte do Grão Mogor*, p. 139.) On the 16th of December, 1715, the Viceroy wrote to the chief of Janjira—"It does not seem proper that Your Highness, who is a vassal of the Mughal Emperor and the Admiral of his fleet, should permit the Angria to be an instrument of his (Mughal Emperor's) subjects' ruin. You saw him with your own eyes enter Colaba with the vessels of Surate he had sieged, without trying to rescue them and fitting your vast fleet for that purpose. And if Your Highness had not cherished so much friendship for this pirate, you would have co-operated with your ships and men for his destruction and ruin when I sent Captain-mor Antonio Cardim against Colaba two years ago. This conduct scandalises all in Asia and particularly me, for in consideration of the amity of the Mughal Emperor, I send a fleet to Surat every year not only for guarding it against any enemy......" (Reis Visinhos, Tomo VII, Fols. 26 and 27). A month later the Viceroy wrote to Asad Ali Khan, offering him naval assistance for the destruction of the Angria. (See Gracias, *Uma*

Dona Portuguesa no Corte do Grão Mogor, p. 156.)

But the Portuguese did not rely on the Muhammadan enemies of Angria alone. Though originally a partisan of the Kolhapur claims, Kanhoji had lately been induced by Balaji Vishwanath, the celebrated founder of the Peshwa family, to offer his allegiance to Shahu and swear fealty to him. This naturally incensed his former patron, the Chhatrapati of Kolhapur, and he willingly concluded an alliance on the 23rd March, 1716, with the Portuguese, to punish this defection as the principal clauses quoted below will show.

1. That Sambhagy Raze will wage by land and sea (all possible) war against the Angria to take from him all the fortresses he holds as a rebel chief in the coast of the North, particularly the fortress of Griem (Gheria or Vijayadurg) which belongs to the said Sambhaji, and for effecting this object the (Portuguese) State will assist him with Men-of-War.

4. That the ships of this state and its subjects shall be able to navigate freely without being seized by the ships of Melondim, and so that there may not be any deception, they shall navigate with passports: those of the North with the passports of the General of that region or of the Captains of the strongholds or fortresses of that coast; those of Goa with the passports of the Government; and those of the South with the passports of the Captains and Factors. The same practice will be pursued with regard to ships from ports belonging to Sambagy Raze, that

may come to trade with the ports of this state, carrying Cartazes as is the practice. And neither our nor Sambagy's ships will pay anchorage (a duty imposed on ships for anchoring in a harbour).

6. That if Sambagy Raze wages war against the rebel Angria and needs powder and ball and wants to purchase the same of this state, the Government will send him all (powder and ball) that it (can spare).

9. That this state shall give Cartaz to a ship of Sambagi Raze, with license to bring horses from Bassora or Congo. It will take a certificate of the Factor that this state has in that port; for if it appears that horses have been embarked at Congo or Bassora and the ship has not brought such a certificate it may be seized as forfeited, for it will then be assumed that horses have been embarked at a port belonging to the Imam of Muscat with whom this state is at war."

This treaty was signed and ratified by one Hari Pant on behalf of his master with the exception of one clause only, which was left for the decision of the Chhatrapati.*

It does not appear that this new alliance had the desired effect, for Sambhaji of Kolhapur was

* Condicoes com que Sambagi Raze ratifica a paz e amisade que tinha com o Estado, violada por alguns dos seus Capitaes dos fortalezas dos portos de mar, principalmente pelo Capitao e Governador da fortaleza de Melondim.—Biker, Tomo VI, pp. 2-4

hardly competent to deal with a "maritime power which had defied the efforts alike of the Portuguese, Dutch and Mahrattas." The Angria's fleet rode the sea boldly seizing merchantmen of all nationalities and the Goa Government had to look for new allies more powerful and more resolute than the Siddi of Janjira or the powerless potentate who then occupied the throne of Kolhapur.

The Portuguese were not the only European nation whom the Angria had offended, the Dutch and the English merchantmen also had suffered at his hands and they made repeated attempts to reduce his power and destroy his fleet "In November 1712, Kanhoji captured the (English) Governor of Bombay's armed Yacht, together with the *Anne* Ketch of Carwar." About the same time he had inflicted serious loss on a Portuguese fleet and the Portuguese at once wrote to the Bombay Government proposing a joint attack on Angria. Govermenor Aislabie preferred peaceful negotiation and declined their offer. Kanhoji was either pacifically inclined or he dreaded an Angio-Portuguese alliance and friendly relations were soon established between him and the English Government of Bombay. Peace however did not last long and the Angria again resumed his hostilities. Aislabie's successor, Charles Boone, was a man of more resolution and warlike disposition. On his arrival at Bombay he set himself to the difficult task of rendering the Indian Ocean safe for the East India Company's ships and fitted out a fleet for the annihilation of

Angria and other sea powers of the Malabar coast. As a detailed account of Boone's expeditions is available to all English-knowing readers in the pages of Downing, Low and Biddulph, it is needless to repeat it here; it may be mentioned that his efforts met with no more success than those made by the Dutch and the Portuguese before him. In 1721 a squadron under the command of Matthews arrived at Bombay. Matthews was a naval leader of considerable experience and had served in Europe under Admiral Byng. His presence at Bombay naturally infused fresh enthusiasm and vigour into the heart of the Bombay government and they decided to make fresh attempts against the Angria and recover their lost prestige. But their recent experience had taught the English seamen to respect the Angria's power and ability and they deemed it unwise to launch upon a fresh enterprise against his seagirt rocky strongholds single-handed. Seven years previously Governor Aislabie had rejected the proffered co-operation of the Portuguese. But in 1721 his successors had grown wiser and had concluded an offensive and defensive alliance with the Goa Government against their common enemy the Maratha Admiral of Colaba. The full text of the treaty has been published by Biker and an English translation is appended below.*

1. There will be an offensive and defensive alliance in this (continent of) Asia against all Asiatic

* Biker, Tomo III, pp. 242-244.

(powers) that may be enemies of the two crowns of Portugal and Great Britain, except the Mughal Emperor and the kings of Persia, Arabia and China. The two nations will immediately commence a vigorous war against the Angria. In concluding any treaty the Angria will not be heard and neither of the allies will listen to anything touching peace unless the term proposed is simultaneously presented to both the allies and nothing will be decided without the compliance of both the nations.

2. If in a given case the enemy of one of the two crowns happens to be the friend of the other, the alliance will be only a defensive one. But neither party should fail on any pretext to help the other when attacked in case of any invasion.

3. As regards the union of the British and the Portuguese forces for operation by land as well as by the sea, the same rule will operate between the two powers as was followed in the last war against Spain, to wit, the Generals of the two nations shall command on alternate days, provided that the Viceroy does not come to the camp and in the same manner the troops of the two crowns shall occupy the place of honour, one in one battle-field and the other in the next.

4. That the auxiliary troops that may be sent for succour (reinforcement) in all detachments and on all occasions of fighting shall be commanded by officers holding higher commissions whether they are English or Portuguese

5. The auxiliary troops shall be paid and maintained by their own sovereign as well on land as in the sea.

6. That all that may be captured in this war in the sea by the two allied nations on the same occasion, shall be by them divided [not excluding] even the munitions and things of importance, the said spoils being first conducted to a port in the Portuguese dominion, and next to a port in the dominion of Great Britain, and all other things will go alternately (to the ports of the Portuguese and the English). The same practice will be pursued on the land only with this difference that the spoils will be taken to the camp where everything except cattle will be equally divided between the two nations. The cattle will be divided by the officers and soldiers of the two nations.

7. That in case goods belonging to any of the (two) nations enter the ports or strongholds that may be taken from the said enemy (Angria), they will not pay duties for the commodities they may carry there, but duties will be taken only for what is sold in the said ports and strongholds.

8. That each nation shall put in the field two thousand infantry with officers in proportion, and with cavalry that may be ready. If necessary a bigger body of infantry will be put in the field by both the parties. In the sea five Pals will be put by each side with smaller vessels as may be necessary.

9. Each corps whether on land or on the sea shall spend (use) munitions on its sovereign's account. In case one of them requires while the other possesses it, the necessary quantity shall be given at a just price.

10. That the fortress of Colaba and the district under its jurisdiction shall belong to the Crown of Portugal, the subjects of Great Britain shall maintain there a house like it (the fortress?) The fortress of Griem and the district under its jurisdiction shall belong to the Crown of Great Britain and the subjects of the Crown of Portugal shall maintain there a house like it. In case the subjects of the Crown of Great Britain desire to demolish the said fortress of Griem, it will be done by both the nations and in that case the artillery and the munitions shall be partitioned by the two nations and an equivalent (share) will be given to the subjects of Great Britain out of Colaba and its jurisdiction, in which the Island of Candrim (Kenery) will be counted.

11. That all soldiers who may desert from one dominion to the other shall be restored without taking them into service. More than one representation from the governor of the country whence they have fled to the governor of the country where they have fled, forgiving the deserters their offence will be necessary for their restoration.

12. If spoils are taken from the country of either of the nations, they shall be after proper proofs have been produced at once restored to the owner.

13. That those deserters, who may seek the protection of either of the crowns, after committing in the country they had left a capital offence, shall not be restored.

14. That after these fourteen articles of alliance have been ratified, the execution of the project will be undertaken, reserving for Their Majesties of Portugal and Great Britain for ever all the rights they claim.—Goa, 20th August, 1721, João Rodrigues Machado.

Biddulph writes: "Long before Matthews' arrival, negotiations had been opened between the Portuguese Viceroy, Francisco José de Sampaio e Castro, and the Bombay Council for a joint attack on Colaba. Through the management of Mr. Robert Cowan, who had been deputed in March to Goa for the purpose, a treaty of mutual co-operation had been drawn up by which the Bombay Council undertook to furnish two thousand men and five ships. The Portuguese authorities undertook to furnish an equal force."

But the joint expedition was not destined to achieve better success. The morale of the Bombay men "habituated to defeat in their attacks on Angrian strongholds" was naturally not very high. The first serious reverse so infuriated Matthews, always violent and overbearing. that he threw the whole blame on his Portuguese allies and wantonly insulted the General of the North. His demeanour towards the Viceroy could hardly be called courteous or even polite. It is needless to say that the highly bred and proud Portuguese officials could not tolerate the ill-manners of the English Commodore. "A little more enterprise on the part of the Mahrattas," observes Biddulph, " would have destroyed the whole force."

Kanhoji was not a mere seaman, he was a diplomat of no mean ability and he did not fail to exploit the difference among his enemies. We are told by Biddulph—" Angria saw his opportunity of breaking up the alliance and opened negotiations with him. On the 17th, the Viceroy wrote to the English, proposing a suspension of arms. With a bad grace they were obliged to consent, seeing in the negotiation, which was against the compact that neither should treat separately, further confirmation of their suspicion of treachery. Angria granted the Portuguese full reparation for injuries, and formed an offensive and defensive alliance with them. The English were left to shift for themselves. Full of wrath, they embarked at once, and sailed for Bombay on the 28th."

Let us now hear the other ally. On the 14th September, 1722, the Viceroy Francisco José de Sampaio e Castro addressed a letter to the King of Portugal about the war with the Angria in which he offers the following explanation for his failure :*

" As the Angria got the information (of the intended expedition) months before (it was under-

* Biker, Tomo III, pp. 300-301.

taken), he opened his treasury and invited his relatives and allies, who are more powerful than he and solicited Shahu Raja (son of Sambagi who, in the days of Viceroy Conde de Alvor, waged a cruel war simultaneously against Goa and its islands, Salcete* and Bardes, and all our strongholds of the North) (to help him). Before I reached Chaul, Pilagi Zadô (Pilaji Jadhava) came to help him with two thousand cavalry besides a force of infantry. Notwithstanding his opposition, I fixed my camp and fought several actions with reciprocal fortune inclined to our favour. A few days after seven thousand cavalry arrived with Baji Rao, the Generalissimo of Shahu Raja, and subsequently more cavalry came and their number exceeded twenty-five thousand. No pitched battle was fought between the two armies not only because I was laid down with a severe fever that then raged in our camp and which aggravated so much that I was compelled to withdraw to my ship, but also because the said Generalissimo invited me to conclude a peace. In these circumstances, as his army was much bigger than ours, and I was in the above mentioned condition, I considered it prudent to accept his proposal and I concluded the treaty (with articles) a copy of which is herewith sent. The said Baji Rao, perhaps at the instance of the Angria, was unwilling to conclude a treaty with the English and I did not come to terms with the Angria directly but with Shahu Raja."

* This is different from Salsetto near Bombay.

So the Viceroy had observed the letter of the treaty of alliance though it was certainly violated in spirit, but probably he had no other alternative. He was no friend of the Angria and long before the joint expedition was ready, Angria had sent him a proposal of peace through the General of the North.* Had he been so inclined the Viceroy could certainly secure favourable terms without shedding a drop of Portuguese blood and without spending a *rei* of Portuguese money. His sincerity therefore was above suspicion. A student of Maratha History cannot but take notice of one fact in this connection. Whereas Balaji Baji Rao invited the English to join him in an expedition for the ruin of Tulaji, son of Kanhoji, Baji Rao stood firmly by Tulaji's father when attacked by the allied Anglo-Portuguese army. Both the chiefs still remembered that they served a common master and the same empire.

After Kanhoji's death, the reputation of his house was maintained by Shekoji, Sambhaji, Tulaji and Manaji. But there was no unity among the brothers and their disunion ultimately caused their ruin.

From a manuscript in the public library of Evora quoted by Ismael Gracias in his *Catalogo dos Livros do Assentamento da Gente de Guerra que veio do Reino para a India desde 1731 até 1811* it appears that a Portuguese fleet that had left the mother country in the previous year encountered in

* Danvers, Portuguese in India, Vol. II, p. 391.

1739 Sambhaji Angria's fleet of seven Pals and ten Galvats and inflicted a defeat on it near the southern coast 13′-54″. Marquis of Louriçal reported on the 3rd January, 1742 another victory against Sambhaji's fleet on the 22nd of November, 1741. In the same letter the Marquis tells us that a vessel belonging to Labourdannais's squadron was captured by the Angria while going south from Goa and conducted to Rajapur. These victories however did not render the sea sufficiently safe for Portuguese merchantmen, for in 1740 the Angria had destroyed a Portuguese fleet (Diogo da Costa, *Relação das Guerras da India*, quoted in Teixeira de Argao's *Descripção das Moedas*, Tomo III) and on the 12th of September, 1744, the Senate of Daman represented to the Goa authorities that they were suffering terribly on account of the Angria's depredations. (Moniz, *Noticias Documentos para a Historia de Damão*, Tomo I). So many naval actions between the Portuguese and the Angria's fleet are mentioned, that space forbids even a brief notice of them here.

But it will be a mistake to think that the Angria brothers had always been unfriendly towards the Portuguese. With the death of Kanhoji and the gradual transfer of the Chhatrapati's authority to the Peshwa's hands, the relation between the hereditary Admiral and the hereditary Prime Minister became more and more strained. It appears from the letters in the eighth volume of the *Livros dos Reis Visinhos* that while Chimnaji Appa was engaged in the memorable siege of Bassein both Manaji and Sambhaji were carrying on friendly correspondence with the Portuguese, and there is reason to believe the Portuguese got from time to time welcome supplies of provision from Sambhaji. On the 2nd of December, 1741, the Marquis of Louriçal wrote a letter to Sambhaji Angria evidently in response to his request for the conclusion of a treaty of alliance.

"The letter, dated the 12th of November, that I received on the 25th of the same month, gave me much pleasure as I found that Your Honour remembers the friendly relations that existed between me when for the first time I governed this Majestic State and your father the great Canogi Angria and as in those days I had so many experiences of the firmness of his word I hope that Your Honour also will show the same fidelity and sincerity that I may on my departure convey to the feet of the throne of the King of Portugal my master." The Viceroy requested Sambhaji to depute a reliable person to Goa (who will always be well received) for concluding a treaty against their common enemies. (Reis Visinhos, Tomo IX, fol. 148.)*

From Sambhaji let us turn to his brothers Tulaji and Manaji of whom we find the following estimate in the Report of the Marquis of Alorna.

"The Angrias.........by their piracies rose to such power that to-day they are dreaded and respected by all. These two brothers (have) divided their

* Volume IX of Reis Visinhos is so much damaged that only a few letters could be with difficulty deciphered.

dominion in two parts. The first called Tulagy Angria who has made his headquarters at Gheria is the nearest neighbour to Goa and is very powerful. The second called Managy Angria has established himself at Colaba near Bombay. The latter (who) is near the Province of the North, has his dominions encircled by the possessions of Nana and has always solicited our friendship and desires anxiously that we should recover that province so that he may have in us a better neighbour than the Marathas from whom he has received continuous insults. Since I arrived here, there was not a single occasion when he did not offer me his maritime forces for some enterprise principally against Nana. Never did I give any positive reply nor omit to thank him for his good wishes and I was keeping up friendly correspondence with him. I did not (venture to) enter into negotiations with him, for I happened to know that he is always drunk and does not know how to read or write. All his negotiations are made through his Brahmins who dominate and hoodwink him, for he cannot by himself examine or decide them, and any negotiation, had it been proposed to him, would be known to Nana through these (same) Brahmins. In these circumstances, I do not know under which class, that of friends or that of enemies, to place this chieftain, but it is safest to count him a neutral so long as his difference with Nana lasts.

During the last four years Tulagy Angria has proposed peace on several occasions for seeing the fair success that Divine Providence gave us against the

Bhonsla, he proposed to me that we should both unite to attack the common enemy. I replied that if through God's grace we had obtained what we wanted without his help, we needed it much less now. When the French squadron came to winter in this port, he feared that we might come against Gheria in alliance with the French and persistently repeated the same proposal and further extended it so that he not only solicited peace with us but also wanted that I should act as a mediator for the treaty that he contemplated with the French. From this I perceived that in this proposal it was fear that prompted him rather than a desire for peace.

When reinforcement arrived in 1748, supposing it of greater strength than it really was, he urged me anew for an alliance soliciting from me help for a united attack on the fort of Monsurem, which place the Bhonsla had taken from him by surprise a short while ago, and desiring that I should sell him the stronghold of Neutim, and the Kailim river which he had lately conquered. This proposal I at once rejected on various pretexts, for the place is only ten leagues from the Bar of Goa and because the neighbourhood of the Angria is more perilous than that of the Bhonsla. I listened to his other proposals being certain that they would have no effect. I replied that as the expedition would be to his interest only and not to ours, he must pay the expenses of the fleet and the munitions. He generously said that he was ready to meet all the costs and enquired about the amount to remit it. I asked of him two hundred thousand rupees to which he replied that he would at once put himself in the field in order to march, that I should send the reinforcement, and added that what touched the payment of expenses between friends could be adjusted after the action, which was the most clever way of saying that he would not pay anything. and as I perceived this I kept him in suspense about this negotiation without definitely concluding it either way. In the meantime he paid our vessels some attention. His envoy is actually waiting for our answer and the final conclusion (of the treaty). Your Excellency will find the proposal for peace he made in the Secretariat and whatever it may be, Your Excellency may be sure that it will not have more duration, firmness and subsistence than the opportunity it offers to the interest of this chieftain and whatever may be the promises and oaths of treaty there is no faith nor law that predominates his convenience."

The Marquis counselled his successor to advance a loan to Tulaji and thereby purchase the security of the Portuguese merchantmen.

Apart from the drunkenness of Manaji and the untrustworthiness of Tulaji there was another impediment, by no means trifling, that stood in the way of a Portuguese alliance with the Angrias against the dreaded Peshwa of Poona. By the fifth article of their capitulation in 1740 (of Bassein) the Portuguese had undertaken to help the Peshwa with their fleet if he waged a war against the Angria.

A treaty was concluded with Tulaji five years after the Marquis of Alorna's departure from India, on the 5th November, 1755. Tulaji stood in sore need of an ally, as the Peshwa was determined to effect his ruin. The Angria chieftain tried his best to conciliate the English at this crisis, but the Bombay Government, now conscious of their increased strength refused to 'take passes of any Indian nation.' Tulaji had no other alternative but to turn to his other European neighbour the Portuguese and his approaches were not repulsed by the ruling Viceroy, the Conde de Alva, the only Portuguese Viceroy who was killed in action on the Indian soil. A treaty was accordingly concluded. The text may not prove altogether uninteresting to a student of Maratha history although the purport of the treaty is already well known.

I. The Most Illustrious and the Most Excellent Sr. D. Luiz Mascarenhas, Conde de Alva, Viceroy and Captain General of India, having attended to the demonstration with which His Highness Tullagi Angria Sarquel sent to represent what pleasure he will derive from peace and amity with the Majestic State and having expressed his genuine repentance for the past discords has forgotten them all and conceded to him (Angria) his (Viceroy's) protection and support.

II. To prevent the peril with which His Highness (O Grandioso) Tullagi Angria Sarquel finds himself threatened in (his) war with Balaji Baji Rao, the Most Illustrious and the Most Excellent Sr. Count Viceroy grants him a reinforcement of five hundred men to be employed principally in the defence of his stronghold and to be quartered in his Capital at Griem, and never on any occasion should the corps of reinforcement be separated without the order and consent of its Commandant.

III. His Highness Tullagi Angria Sarquel will pay the same troops punctually through this state in accordance with the lists of pay that will have to be given him by the Matricula geral of the State, copies of which will be taken by the Commandant.

IV. He is equally bound to quarter the troops with all possible convenience in the fortress of Griem, in separate places from Hindus and Muhammadans, in conformity with the mode of living of the Christians, and they will have the necessary liberty for the exercise of the Catholic religion and the cult Divine.

V. The necessary foods and provisions will be supplied them at the order of His Highness Angria Sarquel at the price current in this city of which an authentic report also will have to be submitted and as porks, kids, wheat, baked rice (arroz cozido) and coconut oil cannot be obtained in his territories, these will be transported from this city to the said stronghold in a corresponding ship supplied by His Highness Tullagi Angria Sarquel.

VI. Payment shall be made to the officers of the troops in this city to enable them to purchase necessary provision for their subsistence and it shall be transported in accordance with the preceding article. His Highness Tullagi Angria shall be obliged to receive all our munitions and to return the same quantity without any diminution.

VII. His Highness Tullagi Angria shall pay to the Fazenda real two lakhs of Rupees.

VIII. To assure the last and other articles of the treaty discussed, the abovementioned envoys shall remain as hostages in the city till the return of the troops that may be sent as reinforcement at the end of the present summer.

IX. On the payment of the first (instalment of) one hundred thousand Rupees in the Fazenda real the Majestic State shall immediately send one company of Grenadiers to reinforce the said stronghold of Griem, and on the payment of the second (instalment of) (the same sum of) one hundred thousand Rupees at the latest twenty days after (the first payment) as His Highness Tullagi Angria Sarquel is bound (to make), the rest of the reinforcement shall go.

X. The Portuguese will not fight with the English in the sea to effect the introduction of these troops in the stronghold of Griem, for that will be an infraction of the peace existing between the Portuguese and the English both in Europe and in Asia.

XI. Another copy of this treaty shall be made with the same terms and after both have been confirmed by signatures and seals, one shall be sent to be kept in the Secretariat of the Majestic State and the other shall be sent to His Highness Tullagi Angria Sarquel, having in this form settled about the despatch of the auxiliary troops the benefit of this treaty will be an efficacious means for a firm friendship between the contracting parties. Drawn in the Secretary of State's office and signed on the 5th of November, 1755. Seal of the Royal Arms. Belchoir José Vaz de Carvalho. Ramagi Ráo Rane, Canó Panta—Custangi Zaetapurcar.*

In the negotiations of this treaty one Ismael Khan (possibly the Governor of Goddo mentioned by the Marquis of Alorna) seems to have played an important part. (See Tulaji's letters, Biker, Tomo VII, pp. 39-42.)

The treaty was signed on the fifth of November and it speaks volumes for the efficiency of the Peshwa's intelligence department that he obtained so early information about it that he was able to send a protest on the ninth, only four days later. To this protest the Viceroy replied in the following manner on the 4th January, 1756 :

" The news of Your Highness (literally great friend) are always pleasing to me. Tuca Sinay has communicated to Your Highness all the circum-

* Biker, Tomo VII, pp. 36-38.

stances that led to the proceedings in which Tullagi Angria solicited the protection of the Majestic Estate. I did not permit myself to be persuaded of his friendship, nor did I desire to prepare a way that might alter the amity and good relations that the Majestic State has with Your Highness, and while the cause would not be justified, the knowledge of Tullagi Angria's lack of faith is enough for me. He has kept his faith in a manner as has compelled me to order the return of the few persons that I sent him for guarding his family and (to direct) that they may return in such a manner, as he had often indicated to me, to avoid during their passage any molestation for stopping this small favour, that in no way will they oppose the progress of Your Highness. You may remain sure that I, on my part, entertain an equal desire for our friendly relations which may daily increase and augment more and more."

On the same date a letter was addressed to the Peshwa by the Secretary of State in which he said :

" As regards the information sent by the Captain in the Angria's (territories) to Your Highness that the Majestic State has despatched a reinforcement to the said Angria for the defence of his lands, I can assure you that there is little truth in it. Even the guard that Ismal Can has sent to the abovementioned Angria was only for the defence of his family on the express condition that they will not fight against the troops of Your Highness or of any other Captain who is in peace with us."

On the 29th of January Tulaji was informed by the Count of Alva that as the articles of the late treaty were not being loyally observed by the Angria, the alliance should be considered to have come to an end.

In the same year the Peshwa's General with his English allies invaded Tulaji Angria's territories. Gheria was captured by the English and Tulaji surrendered to the Marathas. The Peshwa contributed to the downfall of the Maratha naval power. The Maratha banner was no more dreaded in the sea and the name of Angria became only a legend and the sovereignty of the sea so long contested by Kanhoji and his valiant sons definitely passed into the hands of a power who half a century later occupied Poona and pensioned off the ruling Peshwa.

The Colaba branch of the Angria family still continued to enjoy their feudal rights and privileges and they maintained a fleet, but their old prestige was entirely gone with the decline of their power.

In January, 1778 a treaty was concluded between the Goa Government and Raghuji Angria, Lord of Colaba. It shows how anxious the Portuguese were to maintain a friendly relation with Raghuji though he could inflict little loss on the mercantile navy of Portugal.

1. If the fleet of the Majestic State or any men-of-war of the fortresses of Diu and Daman meet the Fleet of Colaba, it will send a small boat to

give information for reciprocal treatment in demonstration of the existing amity.

2. The ships of Colaba shall be able to come freely to this port of Goa and to go to Daman and Diu for the benefit of their commerce, with the passport of His Highness Raghuji Angria, Lord of Colaba, to show that they are his subjects.

3. In the same manner ships belonging to the subjects of the Majestic State, either of this city or of Daman and Diu, shall freely continue their trade with the ports of Colaba with the passport of the State and of their respective government.

4. When by some chance the fleet of Raghuji Angria, Lord of Colaba, comes to this port of Goa or to those of Daman and Diu it will be given a good reception permitting it to purchase at a just price all commodities that it may need, and the same treatment shall be accorded in the ports of Colaba to the fleet and other vessels of Goa, Daman and Diu.

5. If the fleet of Colaba enters any of the ports of Goa, Daman and Diu with any prize ship or other vessels not belonging to the dominions of the Majestic State, no obstruction will be offered and in case the Armada of the Majestic State meets the said Armada of Colaba with such prize in the Southern or the Northern coast, they will hoist their banners and pursue their course after making a signal of a cannon shot and without making any enquiry about each other or about their prize.

6. When His Highness Raghuji Angria. Lord of Colaba, requires the help or assistance of the Majestic State, he will demand and it will be accorded. The Majestic State in its turn will do the same in case it has the same need and the two powers will observe this article with reciprocity.

Two copies of the present treaty will be drawn up with the same terms for being sealed and signed and for reciprocal observance and perpetual fulfilment and for the preservation of a firm amity that should subsist between the two parties, one copy will be sent to His Highness Raghuji Angria, Lord of Colaba, and the other will be preserved in the Secretariat of the Majestic State. Goa, 7th of January, 1778. The Red mark of the Governor, D. José Pedro da Camara.*

The good relation so established seems to have continued undisturbed, for Raghunath was not in a position to pursue the aggressive policy of his famous predecessors. In the 12th volume of the *Livros dos Reis Visinhos* we find a letter addressed to " Grandioso Ragogi Angria Vazarat Mav Sarquel Rezidente da Ilha de Culabo" (Fol. 12) on the 14th December, 1782. We need not quote the whole letter which testifies to the amity that then existed between the Governments of Goa and Colaba. The following extract will illustrate the spirit that runs

* Biker, Tomo VIII, pp. 47-49.

through it : "I am sure that Your Highness will not have to reject the friendship of the Majestic State, that is to the interest of both the parties, till we can submit to His Majesty......more favourable terms according to Your Highness's desire......the decision of my sovereign."

We cannot conclude this section without making a reference to another Angria who bore the same name as the Lord of Colaba. We come across three letters addressed to him in the 11th volume of the *Livros dos Reis Visinhos.* He is differently called Raghuji and Raghunathji, but he is styled as '*Cabo da Armada de Aidar Aly Can*' or Captain of Haidar Ali's fleet. It is possible that a scion of the Angria family had entered Haidar's service after the fall of Gheria. We know nothing however about Haidar Ali's Captain Raghuji. It will be somewhat rash to identify him with the Lord of Colaba. For while the one is distinctly styled as *Cabo da Armada de Aidar Aly,* the other is always mentioned as Lord of Colaba probably to distinguish him from his less exalted namesake. He might be closely related to Tulaji whose line became extinct according to the *Patre Yadi* account. It is needless to say that Haidar would gladly welcome an Angria in his country and put him in charge of his fleet as the reputation of this family of seamen as intrepid naval leaders had spread all over the Deccan.

XI. The Peshwas' Army.

The Portuguese papers could not be altogether silent about the Maratha army. The Marathas were the most formidable enemy they had in India. Chimnaji Appa had conquered Salsette, Bassein and the neighbouring districts from their Portuguese rulers and the papers regarding that campaign published by the Late Sr. Ismael Gracias throw much light upon the military organisation and the military tactics of the Marathas while at the zenith of their power. Quoted below is an estimate of the Maratha army from the pen of an able and intelligent Viceroy, the Marquis of Alorna. It should be noted that the defects of the Maratha military system did not escape this intelligent foreign observer :

" From what experience I have of it, I do not consider that the army of the Marathas and of other princes, that has by rumour such an age-long reputation in this part as in (the rest of) Asia and in Europe, is anything more formidable than a rabble. I would have no hesitation with a corps of five thousand regular soldiers to attack such an army though fifty thousand (strong). The disorder that they have in their army is the same they observe in marching and in encampment. Their army differs little from that of the Gypsies ; each one finds out a place, a shade or a tree that suffices to accommodate him ; they have little vigilance of guards or sentinels and are in this respect very easily (to be) surprised. This militia is divided into three corps, cavalry, infantry and armed elephants. The cavalry is composed of a few good horses and an infinite number of sorry jades called nags. Some soldiers of this corps are armed with lances, others with large swords. The Sipaes of the infantry are armed with Caitocas which is a kind of small firearm carried by them much more frequently than our arms, and some with one or two long and large swords and others with bow and arrow. An infinite number of men called Fakirs always follow the army, who are not men of arms, nor fighters by profession, but who only rob and ravage the country they pass through. The elephants, taught and trained for war, are of the greatest value to the Hindus, when they are intrepid and not afraid of noise. Princes, generals and distinguished persons mount them; they are used to attack the enemy carrying different platoons of men armed with bow and arrow. When infuriated they cause great harm with the trunk. There are elephants (when they have all the necessary qualities) that sell for twenty thousand rupees. These troops are not such as can get a firm footing (against) an enemy, and attack him with an intrepid resolution. All their operations consist in sallies, surprises and ambuscades; and in woods and defiles, supposed to be safe, they are terrible and very formidable on the road (after a rout); finally these troops are a kind of Pendhari with less ferocity and courage but exceedingly cunning to find out any disorder or advantage. The more important of their enterprises terminate more in causing harm, robbery and devastation of the country than in fighting battles decided by sword, by fire, and causing great horror.

The dread that all have for the Maratha spreads before their armies and announces to the provinces through which they pass and at greater distances the loss with which they menace them. This compels them to send immediately emissaries to the armies to escape by (giving) many lakhs of rupees the ruin with which they are threatened. When the expedition is finished, the armies gather without unsheathing the sword, an immense spoil and wealth which at times are not equivalent to the expenses incurred for the allied troops to whom one rupee per day is paid for each man and five hundred rupees for each horse that is wounded, lost or killed in the invasion. If similar troops had discipline and courage in proportion to other circumstances, they would be invincible. None endure so many hardships as these : they do not require military uniforms for they travel naked from waist upward, with three or four *apas*, a kind of cake made of rice or wheat which they get for eating for a number of days and for this reason they are excused from the great embarrassment of carriages that a big army requires for carrying provisions. By extensive and repeated incursions, the Marathas have inspired such terror and panic in the whole of Asia from the Indus to the Ganges that all yield to them and none resists them. Many times they have arrived to touch with their lance the walls of Delhi and Agra, capitals of the Great Mogul. The kingdoms of Cambay and Gujrat, the provinces of Arcot and the Carnatic and all the districts of Bengal have recently been the pitiful theatre of their destructions, whence they have extorted and actually carried away immense wealth thereby making the treasury of the same Mogul diminish considerably."

This is the estimate of the strength and the weakness of the Maratha army that we have from a very shrewd foreign observer whose interest it was to secure reliable and accurate information.

Though the Marathas had their own cannon foundries, they relied more upon a supply of artillery and ammunition from their European neighbours than on their own manufactures. The fifth article of a treaty concluded between the Portuguese Government and the Peshwa Baji Rao on the 9th January, 1722 (just after the joint Anglo-Portuguese expedition against Kanhoji Angria's headquarters) permitted the Peshwa to purchase artillery, ball and powder in Portuguese territories at a just price (Biker, VI, pp. 10-12). Naran Vithal Dumo, the Portuguese agent, was asked by the Poona Government to inform the Viceroy that the Peshwa wanted a supply of big and small bronze cannons of the latest type with necessary munitions, balls and powder in view of the likelihood of a war (Biker, VIII, p. 236). From a letter addressed to Ananda Rao Dhulap on the 2nd September, 1782 (Reis Visinhos, Tomo II, Fol. no. obliterated) it appears that he had asked for a supply of sulphur and the Portuguese authorities had promptly found the quantity required. Parashram Bhau Patwardhan also, while engaged in the siege of Dharwar, had approached the Portuguese authorities at Goa for the munitions he wanted and as the Goa merchants were not then in a position to supply any gunpowder, twenty-five Khandis of powder was given gratis out of the Government stock (Biker, Vol. IX, pp. 212-213). A letter in the tenth volume of the *Livros dos Reis Visinhos* shows that Mahadaji Sindhia also purchased powder from the Portuguese.

But it is not artillery, balls and powder alone that the Marathas purchased from their Portuguese neighbours. In 1760 Peshwa Balaji Baji Rao formed an alliance with the Portuguese for the conquest of Janjira. The Portuguese Government undertook to send at the Peshwa's expense a Portuguese auxiliary force to co-operate with the Marathas in the projected expedition. The Maratha disaster at Panipat saved lucky Janjira from conquest and annexation. During the civil war that distracted Maharashtra after the murder of Narayan Rao both of the contending parties sought military aid from Goa. In a memorial presented to Nana Fadnavis by the Portuguese agent, Narana Rao Vithal, it was mentioned as a proof of their friendship that the Portuguese had refused the assistance solicited by Raghunath Rao and had delivered into the hands of the Maratha authorities Tulagi Panvar, a criminal guilty of ' *lesa magestad.*' (Biker, Vol. VIII, p. 249.) They were willing to assist the ministerial party provided they offered a sufficiently tempting price as we read in a letter addressed to " O Illustre Honorado e valoroso Mhadagy Sindô, Superior de grande Exercito de Milicias " (Reis Visinhos, Tomo II). " In consideration of the amity that prevails between the Majestic State and the Most Felicitous Madou Rao Naraen Pradan, I am prepared to help him against his enemy, His Highness Ragoba, with the troops of the State if the Most Felicitous Peshwa orders the restoration to this State of its ancient dominions, the fortress of Bacaim (Bassein) with all its jurisdiction and all the villages of Daman after a settlement convenient to both the parties " (8th July, 1780). What reply Mahadaji Sindhia, then the mainstay of the ministerial party, vouchsafed to this letter we do not know, but it is apparent that the price demanded by the Portuguese was deemed exorbitant by the partisans of the young Peshwa.

Space does not permit me to quote here the full text of a treaty concluded between the Portuguese and the Peshwa in 1779 when the Poona Government ceded the Pargana of Nagar Haveli to the Portuguese Government. Its terms are somewhat analogous to those of the treaty concluded by the Portuguese with Raghuji Angria, Lord of Kolaba, and provides for reciprocal friendly treatment between the two states and their respective subjects. A Portuguese translation of the original Marathi text by Ananta Camotim Vaga, a Shenvi linguist in the Portuguese service, will be found in *Noticias e Documentos para a Historia de Damão* by Antonio Francisco Moniz (junior) (pp. 207-211).

Most of the treaties that the Portuguese concluded with the successive Peshwas provided for freedom of trade and it appears that the Peshwas' officers did not forget to secure trade facilities for their own countrymen. Thus, the treaty of peace and amity between Senhor M. da Silveiro de Menezes, Captain General of the fortresses and territories of the North and Senhor Chrishna Rao Mahadeo, Governor of Galliana (Kalyan) (1731-1732, 30 January-10 February) not only provided for the free movement of merchantmen but also laid down that after the terms of the treaty had been ratified the merchants of Kalyan and Bhivandi would be allowed to have a bazar in the city of Bassein where they required one for their trade. (Biker, Vol. VI, pp. 175-178.) The following unpublished letter from the 11th volume of the *Livros dos Reis Visinhos* may not prove altogether uninteresting as it tells us how silk and other products of China found their way to the Maratha holy place of Pandharpur through the enterprise of Portuguese and Maratha subjects. " To Naraena Sinay Dumo : Gopala Naique Canado, Bapugi Naique Canado, and Bapugi Naique Parque, merchants of Pandarpur, purchased from the merchants of the State a large cargo of silk and other stuffs of China that the tradesmen of Macau brought to this capital in their boats last year. It did not appear to me that they traded with the English. It is certain that both Macau whence these stuffs came and this city where they were sold belong to the Royal Crown of Portugal. From the representations made by the said merchants I learn that the said stuffs are now deposited at Sangolim. I am writing to the Most Felicitous Madou Rao Narana for permission to disembark them in consideration of the excellent amity that exists between the two powers and to allow the said merchants to carry on their trade in this city. And I direct you to apply to the (Peshwas') Government and urge them to permit the disembarkation of the said stuffs and a Sanad for the same merchants for freely continuing their trade in this city. Goa, 16th October, 1781, F. G. de Souza. (Reis Visinhos, Tomo II, Fol. 125.) A letter, as the above epistle tells us, was written to the Peshwa also and the request of the Portuguese Government was granted (22 February, 1782, R. V. II, Fol. 143).

The Portuguese records do not fail to throw light upon other aspects of the Maratha Government. Their religious policy was liberal and tolerant and Christian subjects in Bassein and other places were permitted to exercise the old rights that they enjoyed under the Portuguese Government. On the 3rd July, 1801, the Sarsubedar of Bassein was informed by the Peshwa Baji Rao II, " The Honourable Vital Rao Gorqui, the agent of the Portuguese Government at Goa, represented to the Government (the Marathi original must be Huzur) at the residence of Poona, that since the District of Bassein passed from the Portuguese Government to that of the Sarkar, the administration of the churches, maintained in this province from ancient times, have been conducted by the Padres and their disciples have been directed and punished in conformity with their religion without any impediment from the Sarkar, and he begged that this order should be sent for the conservation of this practice. We have decided, as the Padres may kill cows, to prohibit that practice entirely. As for the religious usages, the Padres will instruct their disciples according to the observances practised from ancient times and those who do not go to the mass will be punished as in the past without any impediment from Your Honour." (Biker, Tomo X, p. 276.)

Before concluding we may observe that the Portuguese politicians had not failed to find out the real source of Maratha weakness. While Vyankat Rao appeared at Margao, the Portuguese addressed a number of letters to Naro Ram Mantri and they tried their best to exploit the difference that existed among the principal Maratha officers. They even attempted to alienate Shahu from his too powerful Prime Minister. This policy was pursued even after the death of Shahu as we learn from the instructions that the Marquis of Alorna left for his successor. It is no wonder that the Portuguese or the English should try to take advantage of the jealousy and misunderstanding that prevailed among the Maratha chiefs, but it is surprising that not only Naro Ram who had no particular reason for identifying himself with the Peshwa's cause but even Bahiropant Mehendale and Anu Bai, the sister of Baji Rao, should constitute themselves the guardians of Portuguese interest at the Poona Court. Bahiropant Mehendale is styled as "procurador" (Agent or Attorney) of the Portuguese Government at Poona, in a letter of the Secretary of State to Naraena Sinay and also in a letter addressed by Gangadhar Panta, Subedar of Gheria, to the Governor of Goa (Biker, Tomo IX, pp. 176-177). When Tenente Coronel J. Phillipe de Landreset was sent on an embassy to the court of Balaji Baji Rao in 1759, he was told by his official superiors: "you will be assisted at the court of Puna by some persons devoted to the Portuguese Government as well as by Anu Bai, aunt of Nana (Balaji Baji Rao), and her son Naraena Vencata Rao and the Nabobo Mujefarganga and others whom you must treat with the greatest urbanity." (Biker, Vol. VII, pp. 159-165.) On March 1, 1791, Naran Vithal, the Portuguese Agent at Poona, wrote to his employers that the best way of getting anything achieved would be to make presents of precious clothes. This is also confirmed by the evidence of English writers like Fryer and Broughton. The Maratha officer was open to bribe and when he got a present he was quite willing to oblige the party that gave it irrespective of his nationality and without pausing to consider the interests of the State. In short personal interest preponderated over that of the State and as the feudal organisation of the Maratha empire had led to the creation within its fold of a large number of semi-independent states, it steadily declined in power as its solidarity was being unmistakably and quickly impaired.

This report does not claim to be exhaustive and it aspires only to indicate what new light the Portuguese records can throw on Indian History. I examined, as I have previously stated, some of the published records and only one section of the unpublished records preserved at Goa. I had no time to go through the *Livros dos Monçœs*, *Livros dos Pazes* and *Livros dos Cartazes*, but it has been amply demonstrated that the students of Maratha History cannot afford to ignore the original Portuguese sources and as very few of these records have hitherto been published, the Portuguese archives still offer a fruitful field for study and research to all students of modern Indian History.

HINDUISM AND MUHAMMADAN HERETICS DURING THE PATHAN PERIOD

The Timuride princes of Delhi were good Muhammadans but during their long sojourn in India they had imbibed many of the superstitious beliefs of the original Hindu inhabitants of the country. Their belief in astrology was probably characteristic of that age, but Sir Thomas Roe, the English ambassador at the Court of the Emperor Jahangir, speaks of one superstitious rite that is still current among the native Hindus and was undoubtedly of Hindu origin. Writes Sir Thomas Roe*—" Then the king descended the staires with such an acclamation of health to the king, as would have out-cryed cannons. At the staires foote, where I met him, and shuffled to be next, one brought a mighty carpe, another a dish of white stuffe like starch into which he put his finger. and touched the fish, and so rubbed it on his fore-head; a ceremony used presaging good fortune." In that " mighty carpe " and " a dish of white stuffe like starch " it is not difficult to identify a *Rohit* fish and a pot of ' *Dadhi*,' things of good omen that every orthodox Hindu likes to touch and look upon when he sets forth from his home for a new place, even to-day.

* Purchas, His Pilgrims, Vol. IV p. 376.

The Hindu and Muhammadan had lived side by side for so many centuries that they had naturally learnt to tolerate and unconsciously imbibe each other's social customs, common beliefs and even superstitious rites, and the process must have begun long before the conquest of India by Babar and his immediate successors. Towards the Tughlak period, the Muhammadans of India had earned such a notoriety for their heathenish practice among their co-religionists outside India that Timur regarded his invasion of India as a real Jehad; according to him most of the Indian Muhammadans were no better than heathens. In the *Malfuzat-i-Timuri* we read that the expedition was directed mainly against "the infidels and polytheists of India." The Muhammadans were neither infidels nor polytheists but the same authority informs us that in this country "there were those who called themselves Mussalmans but had strayed from the Muhammadan fold." (Elliot and Dowson, Vol. III, p. 426.) In the defence of Bhatnir the Muhammadans not only fought side by side with their Rajput comrades and fellow countrymen but, like them when all hopes were lost, killed their women and children and rushed forth to fight and die sword in hand. Evidently, the Hindus and Muhammadans had learnt to unite in the face of a common danger and disaster. Both of them had learnt not only to tolerate but to co-operate with each other and from the evidence at our disposal it appears that the social customs and even religious beliefs of the Islamic conquerors of India did not long remain unaffected by those of their Hindu subjects and neighbours.

A zealous Muhammadan was Firuz Shah Tughlak. In his reforming zeal he did not spare either himself or his subjects, and heresy, wherever and whenever detected, was sternly suppressed. He has given us a list of his achievements in a short work called *Futuhat-i-Firoz Shahi* and this gives us some idea of the encroachment made by Hinduism on the Muslim mind in those days. Firuz Shah informs us—" There was a sect of heretics who laboured to seduce the people into heresy and schism. They met by night at an appointed time and place, both friends and strangers. Wine was served, and they said that this was their religious worship. They brought their wives, mothers, and daughters to these meetings. The men threw themselves on the ground as if in worship, and each man had intercourse with the woman whose garment he caught. I cut off the heads of the elders of this sect and imprisoned and banished the rest so that their abominable practices were put an end to." We know nothing more about this heresy suppressed by the pious Emperor but from the short description of their abominable rites one feels tempted to find in these heretics the Muhammadan converts of *Tantrism.* The free use of wine and communion of women at their place of worship reminds us of the well-known *Bhairavi-Chakra* of the Tantrists.

If the *Tantras* found their votaries among Indian Muhammadans in those remote days, the ordinary idolatrous practice was not without its admirers among them. We read in the pages of *Tarikh-i-Firoz Shahi* of Shams-i-Siraj Afif, of a Brahman who perverted the Muhammadan women of Delhi and led them to become infidels. It does not appear possible that the Brahman actually converted these Muhammadan women, for even in those days Hinduism was not a proselytizing religion. All that these female converts to idolatry probably did was to worship a wooden tablet "covered within and without with paintings of demons and other objects." The Brahman was burnt to death after a formal trial by a body of Muslim theologians but the Historian does not tell us whether that served as a deterrent to the fair delinquents of Delhi.

If *Tantrik* doctrines in their grossest interpretation were accepted by some sensualists, and ordinary idolatry, without any philosophy at all, found converts among credulous women, the higher teaching of the Vedanta was not altogether lost upon the Muhammdans of India. Sufism is, as is well known, nothing but Vedantism in its Islamic garb and the celebrated Shaikh Nizamuddin Aulia was suspected to Sufi leanings. Sufism, however, did not disappear with him and was found to prosper in its most advanced form during the reign of Firuz Shah in the far-off province of Gujrat. The Emperor tells us—A person...set himself up as a Shaikh in the country of Gujrat, and having got together a body of disciples, used to say, "*Ana-l-Hukk*" (I am God). He commanded his disciples that when he used these words, they were to say " thou art, thou art!" He further said, " I am the king who dies not." In the above-mentioned exclamation—" Ana-l-Hakk " we hear nothing but an echo of " So'ham " (" I am He ") and the Hindu theory of identity and unity between the Creator and his creation. A book written by the Gujrat heretic was burnt by the orders of the zealous Emperor, but did that root out this heresy?

The Emperor also tells us that " A custom and practice unauthorised by the Law of Islam had sprung up in Mussalman cities. On holy days women riding in palankins, or carts or litters, or mounted on horses or mules, or in large parties on foot, went out of the city to the tombs." This new practice did not meet with the Emperor's approval and he frankly informs us that it has not the sanction of the Law of Islam. Were these Muhammadan ladies emulating the example of their Hindu sisters who were in the habit of going to holy cities on pilgrimage on festive occasions in large companies attended by only a comparatively small number of the male sex?

It may be objected that these heretics were probably new converts and uneducated people of the lower classes who found it very difficult to shake off their old beliefs and customs. This objection is not unreasonable and from the meagre materials now at our disposal it cannot be satisfactorily answered. But it is noteworthy that during the reign of Sikandar Lodi, a Muhammadan nobleman of very high station and probably of good education as well,

Ahmad Khan, son of Mubarik Khan, Governor of Lucknow, was accused of becoming a convert to the Hindu doctrines. Probably this conversion did not go further than an avowed sympathy as in the case of Prince Dara Shuko in a later age, but it is undoubtedly significant. Many Muhammadan scholars studied Sanskrit literature and philosophy. The celebrated poet Amir Khusru, " the parrot of Hind," was a sincere and ardent admirer of both. There is no reason to suppose that he was the solitary Muhammadan to admire the ancient philosophy and literature of the Hindus in Pathan period. The Vedanta and the Upanisads have many European admirers to-day, and is it impossible that they found some real converts among the Muhammadans of those days? It is highly improbable that these heresies would have attracted the attention of the Emperor Firuz, had they been confined among a few low-class renegades newly and probably forcibly converted into Muhammadanism. Either these heretics could count among them men of note or the heresies suppressed by Firuz Shah must have been very widespread indeed. It is not improbable that some men of high rank at least had some leanings towards the heresies described above. Converted Hindus often rose to very high position in the days of the Pathan Emperors. Khusru Khan, the notorious favourite of Mubarik Khilji, was a converted Hindu and so was Khwaja Jahan, the all-powerful minister of Firuz Shah Tughlak. It appears that in those days converted Hindus, even when highly placed, did not forget their former friends and relatives, nor did the latter hesitate to stand by their converted kinsman. In the pages of Ferishta we find an instance of a Hindu chief permitting a brother, converted into Islam, to reside in his fort. Khusru relied mainly on his Hindu friends in his ambitious schemes and so did Khwaja Jehan, the junior. Heredity and environment, after all, cannot be easily dismissed and these highly placed converts, who inter-married in high families were probably not a little responsible for the propagation of the Hindu ideas and introduction of Hindu customs among their new relatives and coreligionists. This seems all the more likely when we remember that to-day uneducated Muhammadans in Bengal willingly worship many popular Hindu gods and the Hindus on their part resort to shrines of celebrated Muslim saints with unmitigated alacrity. Even caste system, a practice opposed to the fundamental democratic doctrines of Islam, is recognised by many Muslims in India. The reforming attempts of Firuz Shah proved a failure, for Sikandar Lodi had to prohibit afresh some of the objectionable practices, said to have been suppressed by Firuz. In the meantime toleration grew apace among the people in general* and in Bengal, in

* The new spirit of tolerance can be illustrated by the following anecdote told by Ferishta: A Muslim holy man once had the temerity to protest against the intolerance of Sekandar Lodi. "He maintained that it was highly improper for a king to interfere with the religion of his sub-

particular, where many Muslim poets came forward to enrich the Vaishnava literature. The Vernacular literature of Hindustan found many Muhammadan

jects, or to prevent them bathing at places to which they had been accustomed to resort for ages. The prince drew his sword and said 'Wretch! do you maintain the propriety of Hindu religion?' The holy man replied, 'By no means: I speak from authority. Kings should not persecute their subjects on any account.'" This offers a remarkable contrast to the opinion, expressed by Kazi Mugheesuddin, when consulted by Allauddin Khilji, that "to slay the Hindus or to convert them to the faith" was a well recognised maxim. But Gulam Hanif forbade heedless execution and commanded that "tribute should be exacted to the uttermost farthing from the non-believers, in order that the punishment may approximate as nearly as possible to death." It is also noteworthy that when a Brahman who claimed equality for all religions was placed before the Kazis of Lucknow (during the reign of Sekandar Lodi) for trial, they were divided in their opinion as to the eligibility of the doctrine upheld by the offender. In an earlier period there would be no difference of opinion among the Muslim Doctors of Law as to the utter worthlessness of any doctrine that placed Muhammadanism and any other faith on the same level. Unfortunately, we have not enough information about such interesting subjects and some side-lights alone were thrown on the state of religious toleration when such a bigot as Firuz Shah deemed it necessary to record what he conscientiously considered to be his services to Islam in India. More tolerant rulers were probably indifferent to heresy and idolatry and only negative evidence of their tolerance is available, except when a Badauni comes to upbraid or an Abul Fazl to eulogize a religious innovator like Akbar.

patrons and towards the close of the Pathan period, the response from the Hindu side was so eloquent that the Muslim rulers no longer felt it necessary to issue bilingual coins. As the Sufis popularised Vedantic doctrines among Muhammadans, so also the Hindus in their turn made a serious endeavour to introduce the democratic principles of Islam into their own faith. The result of this influence was the Sikhism of Nanak and the Vaishnavism of Chaitanya.

When the Muhammadans first came to India the Hindus naturally kept aloof from their conquerors and the followers of the two faiths regarded each other with jealousy and mistrust. But gradually their relation improved and the early Pathans became as much Hindustanis as the Saiyads of Barha in the closing years of the so-called Moghul period. A careful examination of known events shows that the Hindus again began to take a prominent part in the politics of the Pathan empire during its last days. The renegade Hindus naturally led the way but they were in due course followed by unconverted Hindus as well. In the Saiyad days the powerful Hindu Zemindars were no longer indifferent spectators but took active part not only in the petty intrigues which marked that period but also in the administration of the country, and the closing years of Pathan rule was marked by a striking revival of Hinduism. The historians of the Pathan rule in India cannot afford to ignore the fact that the Afghan Jahgirdars of Northern India once looked to Rana Sanga of Mewar for leadership in their opposition to Babar and his foreign hordes. A new spirit of comradeship and sympathy of which the heresies mentioned by Firuz Shah were probably the first fruits, was fast coming into existence when it was interrupted, for a short time only, by the advent of a new band of Muhammadan warriors, yet unaccustomed to tolerate idolatry and unfamiliar with the brighter side of Hindu culture.

THE ENGLISH PROCURATOR AT SHIVAJI'S COURT

In a Portuguese letter addressed by the Secretary of State to Naraena Sinay, the Portuguese envoy at the Peshwa's Court, Bahiropant Mehendale, a distinguished nobleman of the Maratha empire and one who enjoyed not a little influence with the Peshwa, is described as "procurador" (Attorney or Agent) of the Government of Goa. His connection with a foreign government was not only well known but was publicly recognised by the officers of the Maratha State, as is clearly proved by a letter addressed by Gangadhar Panta, Subedar of Gheria to the Governor of Goa (Biker, Vol. IX, pp. 176-177). This comes as a surprise to a student of history to-day, for although it is not unusual in our own time for a subject of one State to hold Consular office for another State, it is unthinkable that a member of one government should constitute himself the special guardian of the interest of another power in his own country. This practice, however, was older than the Peshwa days and prevailed even during the reign of the great Shivaji.

The English East India Company's officers at Bombay sent no less than four ambassadors to Shivaji at different times. Their first envoy or ambassador was Lt. Ustick whose journal is mentioned in a letter written to Surat from Bombay. The journal of Mr. Nicholls has been preserved among the manuscript records now in the India Office. We have but meagre notice in the Factory Records of the embassy of Samuel Austen, the last of the four; but the third ambassador, Mr. Henry Oxinden, was in a sense the most fortunate of them all.* He was present at Shivaji's coronation at Rairi, and as the Surgeon in the Company's employ at that time was a man of literary taste, Mr. Henry Oxinden's account of his journey to Rairi and his activities there was given to the public as early as 1698. Dr. Fryer reproduced Oxinden's Narrative almost word for word. The only change he thought necessary to make was to convert the first person in which the ambassador wrote into the third. But the Marathi names must have puzzled Fryer a good deal, and his spelling of Marathi personal names was mostly wrong. In the Instructions drawn up for Oxinden occurs the following:

"Among Sevagees chiefest ministers of State you must particularly apply yourselfe to Naragy Punditt who hath expressed extraordinary kindness and affection to the Company's interest and therefo(re) you are to communicate unto him all our Desires and proposalls, before they be presented to Sevagee, that you may take his advise and approbation, therein, desiring him to interceed and mediate with Sevagee Rajah for the speady conclution thereof." (O. C., Vol. 35, No. 3963.)

* The journals and reports of Nicholas, Oxinden and Austen have been published by the present writer in his *Foreign Biographies of Shivaji.*

Henry Oxinden calls this minister our procurator and gives a fairly detailed account of his interview with the Brahman (O. C., Vol. 35, No. 3965), Fryer calls him Narranji instead of Naragy and this alteration in the name, slight as it is, has so long stood in the way of a correct identification of this procurator of the English at Shivaji's Court. Dr. Crooke who edited Dr. Fryer's account for the Hakluyt Society, did not think it necessary to compare the published narrative with the manuscript in the India Office and confused the Procurator with Naran Sinay, Mr. Oxinden's interpreter. Mr. Sardesai in his Marathi Riyasat, Vol. I, accepted Fryer's reading as he had no access to the manuscript records. Prof. Sarkar in his *Shivaji* (First Edition, I do not know whether he has made any alteration in the Second Edition) calls him Naraji Punditt and Narayan Pandit.* And recently the greater portion of Oxinden's interesting Narrative has been published by Mr. C. H. Payne in the concluding pages of his *Scenes and Characters from Indian History*. Mr. Payne examined the manuscript records but unfortunately did not preserve the original spelling of place and personal names. He also calls the Procurator Naranji Pandit which was certainly not his name.

* These mistakes occur also in the second edition of *Shivaji and his Times* (p. 339). But since the publication of this paper in the *Calcutta Review* (May 1926) the correct reading of the procurator's name has been adopted in the third edition of Sarkar's *Shivaji* (published in 1929).

It should be noted that the Procurator was one of Shivaji's "chiefest ministers of state," *i.e.*, a member of the Ashta Pradhan Council and I have no doubt that Fryer's Naranji and Prof. Sarkar's Narayan Pandit was really Niraji Raoji, Shivaji's Nyayadhish. The name occurs thrice in the Instructions mentioned above. It is differently spelt as Naragy and Nerajee. Those who are familiar with the old records of those days know that the English scribes of the time were not very careful about their transliteration of Indian names. Shivaji's name was not infrequently written by them as Savage. In Henry Oxinden's Narrative the name has without any exception been always written as Neragy but my identification is based on stronger evidence than the uncertain spelling of the name, though I have not the least doubt about the accuracy of my reading. Naragy or Neragy is mentioned also in a letter written by Naran Sinay, but as the copy now available to us is only an English translation of the original letter written in Portuguese, we do not know whether Naran Sinay's spelling has been faithfully preserved by his translator. The interpreter, however, gives a valuable clue as to the identity of the procurator in the opening para of his letter to his master at Bombay (Factory Records, Surat, 88, Fols. 78-83). He writes :

"I went to Banchar to visitt Naragy Punditt which place is at the mountaines ffoot, and enquireing for him I encountered with his eldest sonne Parlad Punditt who advised me that his father Naragy Punditt was at the mountaines head."

When Oxinden calls him Neragy and Narayan Shenvi informs us that his eldest son was Parlad Punditt (Pralhad Pandit), we may be reasonably sure that the personage réferred to is no other than Shivaji's Nyayadhish, Niraji Raoji, father of Pralhad Niraji the celebrated Pratinidhi of Rajaram, and Shivaji's envoy at the Kutub Shahi Court. Both Prof. Sarkar and Mr. Payne have referred to this letter but they seem to have overlooked this passage while modernising the spelling of Naragy or Neragy's name.*

It may be noted in this connection that the English were anxious to please Niraji as will be evident from the following extract from the Instructions :

" In the agreement made with Sevagees envoy Bimagee Punditt touching the satisfaction to be paide the Company for theire losse at Rajapore in regard Neragee Punditt whom we have recommended unto you did prove the only mediator to bring Sevagee to so fair and good accommodation, we thought good to promise him for his encouragement 500 Pagoths to be paid him out of the said money, thereby to oblige him the more to doe the Company further service in their traide hereafter and also we promised to Bimagee Punditt the envoy for his effectual service, therein 100 pagoths, wherefore in case they desire the

* Probably both of them were misled by the article on Raigad in the *Bombay Gazetteer*, Kolaba Volume.

said money you may confirme our promise; but endeavour to put off to the second or third payment, but if they earnestly press to have it made good out of the first you are not to deny them for it is necessary for us to keep them our friends."

It is needless to point out that the practice alluded to in the above extract will not be tolerated to-day in any civilised country.

THE KARNATAK EXPEDITION

Who planned the Karnatak expedition and with what object? It is not difficult to answer the second question, but to find a definite reply to the first is by no means very easy.

It is generally believed that Raghunath Narayan Hanmante, a masterful man of overbearing temper, quarrelled with his young master Ekoji Bhonsla and induced Shivaji to claim a share of his paternal Jahgir in the Karnatak in order to humiliate the young ruler of Tanjore. This story has been unanimously accepted by practically all modern historians of the Marathas, Grant-Duff, Sardesai, Kincaid and, last but not least, Sir Jadunath Sarkar. The latter gave, in the first edition of his *Shivaji and His Times,* a detailed narrative of Raghunath Narayan's journey from the court of Ekoji to that of Tana Shah, his interview with Madanna Pandit, the all-powerful Brahman Prime Minister of Golkonda, the conclusion of a treaty, or at least an understanding, with him with a view to a joint invasion of the Sultan of Bijapur's possessions in the Karnatak including those of the hated Ekoji and finally the acceptance of this ready-made scheme by Shivaji, who had no particular reason to be swayed by considerations of his step-brother's feelings. All these details are not, however, available in the *Sabhasad Bakhar.* Krishnaji Anant Sabhasad tells us that Raghunath Narayan and his brother Janardan were able men. They could not pull on well with Ekoji and consequently left his service and migrated to Maharashtra, where they were warmly welcomed by Shivaji. When Shivaji proceeded to the Karnatak with a strong force of 25,000 cavalry, he chose Raghunath and Janardan among others to accompany him. Raghunath was afterwards appointed to be the Viceroy of the newly conquered province. This selection was both wise and natural. Shivaji wanted in his war-council a man who was well-versed in the confused and ever-shifting politics of the Karnatak, and Raghunath was eminently qualified for his new office. Sabhasad, however, does not suggest that Raghunath was the real author of the scheme which bore such splendid results at the hands of Shivaji.

The *Shahanav Kalmi Bakhar*, supposed* to be a *contemporary* chronicle, gives a different account. According to it, Raghunath Narayan left Ekoji's

* The *Shahanav Kalmi* or the *Ekanav Kalmi Bakhar*, as it is sometimes called, is not a contemporary chronicle of Shivaji. It mentions the *dutarfa amal* or dual government in Tulapur which refers to the Peshwa period, and it also contains detailed information about Vyankoji's sons. Its chronology is usually faulty, and had the author been a contemporary of Shivaji he would undoubtedly have mentioned the two sacks of Surat. According to him, Shivaji sacked Surat only once and the Karnatak expedition preceded the ceremonial coronation of Shivaji. These glaring inaccuracies lead but to one conclusion, that the chronicle cannot be a contemporary work. Sir Jadunath Sarkar, however, treats it as a contemporary record of Shivaji's achievements, but, as usual, refrains from giving any reason for his conclusion.

court, as the latter preferred to look after his government in person. The discontented Brahman sought service at Bijapur but was induced by Shivaji to repair to Panhala, where the great Maratha leader was at the time. Raghunath Narayan was then appointed Majumdar in the vacancy caused by the death of Nilo Sondev. He then induced Shivaji to claim his rightful share of Shahaji's Jahgir.

It is to be noted that the *Shahanav Kalmi* version differs substantially on some important points from that of Sabhasad, and there are some inherent flaws in the story so commonly and unhesitatingly accepted. In the first place, Ekoji was not the weak and indolent young man he has been represented to be by the later chroniclers. The conquest of Tanjore is commonly ascribed to Shahaji by his panegyrists, but that achievement must go to the credit of his much maligned son. The testimony of the contemporary Jesuit letters on this point is as emphatic as unambiguous, and it is needless to point out that the conqueror of Tanjore could not have been an indolent or unwarlike person. Nor was he loth to look after the administration of his Jahgir. If we accept the evidence of the author of *Shahanav Kalmi Bakhar*, Raghunath Narayan's grievance was based on his exclusion from the government. Ekoji, of course, suffers badly in comparison with his famous step-brother, but had he been willing to while away his time in luxury and indolence, and leave the government in the hands of Raghunath Narayan, the latter at least would have been in no hurry to preach him a sermon on the dignity of kingly office and the duties of a Kshatriya warrior. It should further be borne in mind that in Ekoji's time it was not regarded as a disgrace to serve a Muhammadan master. His father had risen to eminence and distinction in the same service. The idea of nationality and patriotism was yet unborn and many of the well-born and well-placed Maratha chiefs regarded Shivaji as a rebel and miscreant. Shivaji was far in advance of his age, Ekoji was not.

Raghunath Narayan has been credited with great scholarship and exceptional ability. That the man who wrote the *Raj-Vyavahar-Kosh* and was entrusted by Shivaji with the viceroyalty of Jinji was a great scholar and an able officer need not be disputed. But he was hardly qualified, if the current story is to be accepted, to be the mentor of a young and, let us admit, wayward chief. If he sincerely wanted to convert Ekoji to his views and lead him back to the path of duty and rectitude, his object was certainly defeated by his own arrogant manners and disrespectful words. The same mistake was committed by him for a second time when he publicly administered a severe rebuke to Sambhaji. Able as he was, Raghunath Narayan lacked exactly those qualities of sympathy and persuasion which go to the making of a great statesman and successful minister.

Even if it is admitted that an expedition to the Karnatak was first suggested by Raghunath

Narayan, the scheme as it was finally adopted could not be his. According to the chronicles, his sole object was retaliation and he suggested that the principality of Tanjore was Shivaji's *bap-roti* (*Shahanav Kalmi Bakhar*). Shivaji, however, conquered and annexed territories in the Karnatak that never belonged to either Shahaji or Ekoji; and Tanjore, as it was conquered by the latter, could never form Shivaji's *bap-roti*. There was another serious objection against making the right of inheritance a *causus belli* between the two brothers. As Sardesai points out, if Shivaji claimed a share of Shahaji's Jahgir in the Karantak, Ekoji might with equal justice claim a share of his father's old Jahgir in Maharashtra. Sabhasad says that Shivaji demanded from Ekoji his father's *biruds* or insignia of honour and rank. What this demand really signified is not quite clear. But we need not critically examine these excuses of war, its object being our principal concern. We shall later find that neither retaliation nor plunder but permanent annexation formed the real object of Shivaji's Karnatak expedition. It is commonly believed that the views of Raghunath Narayan hardly went beyond retaliation.

The success of this project depended mainly on the co-operation of Golkonda and the temporary inactivity of the Moghul Viceroy, and these demanded diplomatic negotiation. A diplomatic agent or envoy was stationed at the court of Golkonda as early as 1672. Niraji Raoji, the first envoy, was succeeded in that office by his more famous son Pralhad

Niraji. In September 1675 Prahlad Niraji was at Raigad, as we learn from Samuel Austin.* In a letter dated the 20th December 1675, Baron made a reference to a meeting with Annaji Pant near Rajapur. Annaji Pant discussed on that occasion the probability of an expedition to the Karnatak, and it is needless to say that the matter must have been settled long ago in the innermost council of the Maratha hero before one of his principal ministers could discuss it with a foreign trader. We, however, do not know when exactly Raghunath Narayan left Ekoji and went to Shivaji's court. He was not at Raigad at the time of Shivaji's coronation. Sardesai says that Raghunath came to Maharashtra in 1675; but unless we know the exact date of his arrival, we cannot ascertain to what extent he was responsible for the expedition with which his name is so intimately associated. It will not be unreasonable to hold that the expedition had been seriously thought of in the earlier part of 1675, as it was openly discussed by Annaji in November or December of that year. Baron further learnt on that occasion that Shivaji had already sent an ambassador to Golkonda to explain his plans to the Sultan and obtain some money from him. The chronology of this period must be more satisfactorily settled before any definite opinion can be given about the origin of the Karnatak scheme. Shivaji was not a person to be blindly led by others, and it may safely be sug-

* See. Sen, *Foreign Biographies of Shivaji*, p. 471.

gested that the political chaos and anrachy in the Karnatak had already attracted the notice of the ever-vigilant Maratha leader and that the arrival of Raghunath and Janardan had removed what little hesitation he might have felt. Janardan, it may be observed, acted as one of the principal advisers of Shivaji in the Karnatak as we learn from François Martin.

Martin and Langhorne apparently believed that Shivaji had entered the Karnatak as an auxiliary of the Sultan of Golkonda at the invitation of Madanna and then refused to relinquish his conquests when he perceived the weakness of his ally. Governor Langhorne wrote to the English East India Company on the 19th June 1676-1677, "We are now to acquaint you that Sevagee, grown great and famous by his many conquests and pillagings of the Moghuls and Visapour countrys, is at length come hither with an army of 16 or 20 M horse and several thousand of foot, being unfortunately called in by the King of Golkonda or Madanna to help them to take Chengy, Vealour and Pamangonda, the remainder of the sea part of the Cornatt country as far as Porto Novo out of the Visiapour's hands, with title of generalissimo, by which means he has gotten in a manner the possession of this country, the said king having no force to oppose him." The Frenchman goes further and accuses Madanna of deliberate bad faith. The Brahman, he suggests, misled his master with a view to put a fellow Hindu in possession of the rich kingdom of the Karnatak. This suspicion was based on surmise only, and neither the Frenchman nor the Englishman could be in the know. Shivaji had decided to invade the Karnatak long before he met Madanna or received any formal invitation from him.

Until recently there were no two opinions about the real aim and object of Shivaji's Karnatak expedition. It was admittedly an expedition of conquest and annexation. But ten years ago Sir (then Professor) Jadunath Sarkar objected that "It is incredible that a born strategist like Shivaji could have really intended to annex permanently a territory on the Madras Coast which was separated from his own dominions by two powerful and potentially hostile states like Bijapur and Golkonda, and more than 700 miles distant from his capital. His aim, I believe, was merely to squeeze the country of its accumulated wealth and return home with the booty. The partition of his father's heritage was only a plea adopted to give a show of legality to this campaign of plunder."

Sir Jadunath's objections, however, do not bear scrutiny. The Marathas were not strangers in the province Shivaji was going to invade. A fairly large number of Brahman and Maratha officers had served under Shahaji and had settled in the Karnatak for good. A Maratha colony had thus been founded in this province and it was but natural for Shivaji, whose avowed aim was to unite the Marathas under one common banner, to annex the Karnatak which had been practically adopted by Shahaji and his friends as their second home.

The ' strategical difficulties ' of holding a province seven hundred miles away from Shivaji's capital were more fictitious than real. If such difficulties had really been insurmountable, the great empires of the world, both past and present, would never have been founded and the Marathas would never have crossed the Narmada. An uninterrupted communication with the base of operation is all that is needed for a strong power to hold a distant country or province, and Shivaji saw that the intervening districts were reduced and securely held. Sir Jadunath himself points out that " The districts that he retained in Central and Eastern Mysore as the result of his Karnatak expedition, had to be connected with his old dominions by his conquest of the Southern corner of Bijapur." This was effected and " the country was formed into a regular province of Shivaji's kingdom and placed under Janardan Narayan Hanumante as Viceroy."

It may be argued that the policy of annexation was an after-thought and had been suggested by Shivaji's rapid success in the Karnatak. But it is difficult to entertain this objection seriously when we learn from Martin that a large number of Brahmans had accompanied Shivaji in search of employment.*

* " Sivagy sent some Brahmens to all the villages in the country for governing them, the number of these scamps who had followed Sivagy for trying to get some

Moreover Shivaji did not keep the French traders of Pondichery long in suspense about his intention to hold Kranatak for good. In June 1677 Martin sent a Brahman to wait upon the Maratha invader. This envoy had no less than three interviews with Shivaji and he was finally told that a Havaldar would be sent to govern Pondichery before long. " Sivagy assured our envoy," writes Martin, "that we might stay in complete security at Pondichery without taking the side of either party; that if we offered the least insult to his people there would be no quarter for us or for those of our people who were in the factory of Rajapour, that he would send an *avaldar* in a few days to govern Pondichery and that we might have to live with him in the same manner as we had done with the officers of Chircam." This message proves Shivaji's decision to annex and govern the conquered country beyond a shadow of doubt. It should be noted that the above-mentioned interview took place before the reduction of Vellore and while Sherkhan Lodi had not yet been worsted.

The first governor of Jinji under whose jurisdiction Pondichery lay was one Vitthal Pandit. In May 1679 he sent one Ambaji Pandit to assure the French Chief of Pondichery of his protection and amity. In 1681 one Balaji Pandit was Governor of Pondichery and in 1689 one Sheshadri Pandit was

employment is something amazing, they counted...more than twenty thousand." François Martin in Sen, *Foreign Biographies of Shivaji*, p. 297.

appointed to the Havaldarship of that place. Vitthal Pandit held the Subedarship of Jinji till 1686 when he was succeeded in that office by one Anand Rao. He was replaced by Timaji in 1687. Vitthal Pandit seems to have been reappointed to his old post in 1689, but in 1690 we find Timaji Keshava occupying that important office. In December 1690 one Sam Rao acted as Havaldar of Pondichery and he was still serving in that capacity in 1693.*

François Martin, to whom we are indebted for an interesting account of the Karnatak expedition speaks very bitterly about the rapacity, oppression and misrule of Brahman officers of Shivaji. It is needless to say that the relations between the French merchants of Pondichery and the Brahman officers of Shivaji were far from friendly. The French were the old allies of Sherkhan Lodi and were still carrying on friendly correspondence with him. The Marathas consequently treated these foreigners with suspicion and coldness. But Martin applauds their industry in reclaiming waste and uncultivated lands in no uncertain terms. "It must, however, be admitted," says he, "that the Brahmens were more careful in making the lands profitable than those under the government of the Mahomettans had appeared (to us) to be. A number of places around Pondichery, covered with brambles and brushwood

* This list is compiled from *Le Stat General des Presents et depences faitez à Pondichery depuis le 18 8bre 1673 jusquez au 3le aoust 1693*, now in the Archives Coloniales of Paris.

only, of which nobody thought (anything), was reclaimed and these have produood well since." It is needless to repeat that the prompt appointment of Havaldars and Subedars for the government of the conquered country and the reclamation and cultivation of unprofitable waste lands by the Brahman officers indubitably testified to their firm resolution to keep what they had seized. It is, therefore, futile to assert that Shivaji, when he formed an alliance with the Sultan of Golkonda and led a formidable army to the rich lands of the Karnatak, only intended "to squeeze the country of its accumulated wealth and return home with the booty." He wisely annexed this far-off colony, as he had probably foreseen that it might one day serve as a secure place of refuge for his successors. A shrewd and wise statesman like Shivaji would not otherwise run the great risks involved in the invasion of the Karnatak while a strong Moghul army was posted in the Deccan.

HYDER ALI'S FLEET

One of the most formidable enemies the English had in India, was Hyder Ali, the able and energetic ruler of Mysore. He formed a steadfast alliance with the French against their common adversary. His son, Tipu, went farther and opened negotiations with many foreign potentates, Zeman Shah of Afghanistan, the Imam of Muscat and, last but not least, the Sultan of Turkey. His ambassadors received a warm welcome at Versailles and although these diplomatic efforts met with scant success, Tipu could very well claim to be the only Indian prince who took any interest in the world politics of his day. But an Indian ruler could not expect to form an effective alliance with Muscat or Constantinople unless he had a strong fleet at his command. Tipu, it is well known, made an attempt to organise a good fighting fleet, but it will be a mistake to suggest that Hyder had failed to appreciate the value of a powerful navy. His English enemies were strong on the sea, his Portuguese neighbours still relied on their navy in their struggle with Indian states, even the Peshwa possessed a fleet of his own. When the conquest of the Malabar coast put Hyder in possession of the famous ports of that region he naturally aspired to extend his power over the sea, but our knowledge of his naval policy is extremely limited. We know that he had a fleet and we also know that his men-of-war were of no use to him in his war against the English. But when he actually undertook the organisation of his navy and what agencies he employed for this purpose are not generally known. It is, however, not impossible to supplement our meagre knowledge on this subject with some scraps of information from unpublished Portuguese records.

Col. Wilks mentions Hyder's fleet but once. In 1768 the Mysore admiral deserted his master's cause and joined the English.* Low gives the following account of this incident in his *History of the Indian Navy.*† "Early in 1768, the Bombay Government fitted out an expedition, consisting of a squadron of their ships, with four hundred European troops and a large body of Sepoys, to attack Hyder Ali's sea ports on the Malabar coast. The enterprise was completely successful. The expedition first made its appearance off Onore, or Honawar where Hyder Ali, the great ruler of Mysore, familiarly known at this time as Hyder Naick, had begun to prepare a fleet. He had, however, alienated from his interests the captains of his ships by appointing as his admiral Ali Bey,‡ an officer of cavalry, who of course, was totally ignorant of

* Wilks' *Historical Sketches of the South of India* (2nd edition), Vol. I, p. 331.

† Low, *History of the Indian Navy*, Vol. I, p. 153.

‡ Lutf Ali Beg, according to Wilks.

nautical matters. The consequence was that, when the expedition appeared off Onore, Hyder's fleet, consisting of two ships, two grabs, and ten galivats, sailed and joined the English. Onore, and Fortified Island, at the mouth of the Onore river, were captured, and thence the expedition sailed for Mangalore.'' Thus in 1768 his fleet proved worse than useless to Hyder. On land he could hold his own against his enemy but on the sea he had the misfortune of witnessing his fleet going over to the other side. Hyder was not the person to be disappointed by a single disaster, however serious, and we shall see how he made a fresh attempt to recoup his loss and reorganise his navy.

If a contemporary Portuguese letter is to be believed, the numerical strength of Hyder's fleet was somewhat greater than that indicated by Wilks and Low. By 1763 Hyder had risen to sufficient eminence and a short biography of his was forwarded to Lisbon along with a letter, dated the 26th January, 1764. This brief but interesting sketch gives a fairly accurate account of Hyder's conquest of Kanara but does not say anything about his naval power.* In a letter, dated the 23rd September, 1765, we come across the first notice about Hyder's growing power on the sea.† It runs as follows: " The whole of this part of Asia (now) enjoys the

* Archivo Ultramarino, Officios dos Governadores, Maço 2, No. 12.

† Officios dos Governadores, Maço 3, No. 44.

benefit of a peace (which is) insecure, on account of the unbridled ambition of the potentates who rule this area : Our neighbours, the Marathas and Aidar Aly Can concluded it during the last winter, and the freedom, in which the latter is, permits him to augment a fleet which has already begun to cause us some anxiety, and if at present we fear him as a pirate, we have reason to apprehend that time and luck may give him the power to ruin us. We know that his fleet now consists of thirty vessels of war and a large number of transport ships. It is commanded by an Englishman with some European officers." In a letter, dated the 12th December of the same year* we again read of Hyder's increasing maritime power. It will not, therefore, be unreasonable to infer that Hyder first launched his fleet sometime between 1763 and 1765, and like many of his neighbours employed European officers to command his navy. But it is a matter of surprise that his admiral should be an Englishman. Wilks and Low say nothing about the nationality of the admiral who joined the English so readily. Nor do we know whether the Englishman, mentioned in the letter quoted above, continued to hold his command till 1768. But apart from the discontent attributed to the appointment of a cavalry officer to the chief naval command, the ready rebellion and desertion of the fleet may

* Officios dos Governadores, Maço 3, No. 25.

very well be explained by the nationality of the admiral. It may be noted in this connection that not merely the English officers, but European commanders of other nationalities as well, deserted Daulat Rao Sindhia during the second Maratha War. It is not unlikely that Hyder appointed Lutf Ali Beg to the head of his fleet because he could not implicitly trust the commanding admiral who happened to be an Englishman. But this is a mere conjecture.

We learn from a letter* addressed by Jose Pedro da Camara to Martinho de Mello e Castro on the 28th December, 1778, that Hyder was again building a large number of men-of-war and a Dutchman was employed to strengthen the harbour of Bhatkal. The letter deserves quotation : " I should particularly inform you that the Nabobo Aidar Ali, aspiring to make himself as respectable on the sea as he is formidable on land, has ordered the construction of many sailing ships† in all the places of the south coast (which are) big enough for this great work. He has hitherto in the sea or in stocks eight three-masted ships which carry 28 to 40 pieces (of artillery) and a similar number of *Palas*, also in the sea or in stocks, of lesser tonnage. For making a greater progress in the work and to provide necessary accommodation for building and preserving the most powerful fleet in Asia, he began

* Officios dos Governadores, Maço 5, No. 70.

† Embarcaçoens de gavia.

this month to build a stockade above the water line in the gulf of Batical, which is situated near Onore on the firm land to the south, and is very near the island of Angediva, with the intention of constructing a huge mole which will enclose a port, where, (at the full tide) it is said, a large fleet can anchor. The projected work also includes fortification for the defence of the port. It is being at present outlined according to its circuit inland; it will have an enclosure big enough for a large borough for the residence of numerous merchants of all nationalities who are expected to be attracted by the gift of convenient plots of the neighbouring lands and the loan of capital, which will ensure their establishment in that place where large warehouses for storing goods, articles and ammunition for a big marine, and factories for the work of a busy arsenal have been so well planned." The letter proceeds to say that this great work was under the charge of a Dutchman named Joze Azelars, who was originally an ordinary ship-wright in the service of the Dutch East India Company. He professed to be a skilled engineer, when he entered the service of Hyder Ali, and undertook to finish the work in three years at an estimated cost of seventeen lakhs of pagodas. Jose Pedro da Camara, to whom we are indebted for this information, was of opinion that it would be impossible to complete the work in the stipulated period for lack of skilled workmen, and we do not know whether this grand scheme was ever realised.

We read in another letter (in the same bundle), dated the 11th May, 1779, that the work was not progressing satisfactorily. After giving a brief account of Hyder's annexation of the Krishna-Tungabhadra *doab*, the letter proceeds to say, " the mole that the Nabobo planned at Batecal, very near Angediva, is being built very slowly, because the Dutch director of the work encounters difficulties enough in the inlets of the bay and (experiences) greater opposition from the Brahmans who assist him as inspectors or overseers of that work. This is all that I can inform Your Excellency about the progress made by this terrible prince."*

Hyder died in 1782, but before his death his fleet suffered another terrible disaster, as we learn from Captain Low. " In the latter part of 1780, Sir Edward Hughes, while on the West Coast of India, dealt a fatal blow to the rising maritime power of Hyder Ally, against whom we were engaged in a life and death struggle. On the 8th of December, being with his squadron off Mangalore, the principal dockyard and naval arsenal of Hyder Ally, the Admiral saw two ships, a large grab, three ketches, and many small vessels, at anchor in the roads with the Nawab's flag flying on board them. He immediately stood in, and finding them to be vessels of force, and all armed, anchored as close to

* Archivo Ultramarino, Lisbon, Officios dos Governadores, Maço 5, No. 28.

them as the depth of water would allow, and ordered the boats of the squadron to destroy them, under cover of the fire of two ships of the Bombay Marine. This service was conducted with the usual spirit and activity of British seamen, and, in two hours, they took and burnt two ships, one of twenty-eight, and the other of twenty-six guns; one ketch of twelve guns was blown up by the enemy at the instant the boats were boarding her; another ketch of ten guns, which cut her cable, and endeavoured to put to sea, was taken, and the third, with the smaller vessels, were forced on shore, the grab only escaping into the harbour, after having thrown everything overboard to lighten her."*

Thus ended the great projects of Hyder 'Ali, and the naval power of Mysore died in its infancy. Col. Kirkpatrick was of opinion that Hyder had bestowed little or no attention on the organisation of a fleet,† but the Portuguese letters, mentioned above, leave no doubt that Kirkpatrick's conclusion, based on negative evidence alone, can no longer be upheld. The earliest reference to Tipu's fleet was to be found, according to Kirkpatrick, in a letter‡ the Sultan addressed to Mir Ghulam Husain on the 24th September, 1786. The navy, says Col. Wilks, " was not finally organised on paper till 1796, and can

* Low, *History of the Indian Navy*, Vol. I, p. 178.

† *Select Letters of Tippoo Sultan*, p. 415.

‡ *Select Letters of Tippoo Sultan*, p. 414.

20

scarcely be deemed to have had a practical existence."* The maritime hopes of Mysore perished with Hyder, and although Tipu established commercial relations with the Imam of Muscat, he did not succeed where his father had failed.†

---

* *Historical Sketches of the South of India* (2nd edition), Vol. II, p. 267. It is, however, difficult to accept this statement of Col. Wilks. In 1787 an alliance between the Portuguese and the Marathas was proposed against Tipu. Two articles of the draft treaty provided for Portuguese naval co-operation with the Marathas against Tipu's fleet. It is, therefore, clear that Tipu's fleet had a practical existence as early as 1787. Officios dos Governadores, Maço 20, No. 95. Biker, *Tratados da India*, Vol. VIII, pp. 221-222.

† Copies of four letters written at different times to one Raghuji Angria, who is described as Captain of Hyder Ali's fleet, are to be found in the Goa archives. These letters, however, furnish no information about the Mysore fleet except that a Hindu officer once occupied a high office in Hyder's navy.

THE SHRINGERI LETTERS OF TIPU SULTAN

What was Tipu Sultan? A normal man or an abnormal monster? A benevolent king or a sanguinary tyrant? A tolerent ruler or an intolerant bigot? Contemporary opinion was very sharply divided. Kirkpatrick describes him "as the cruel and relentless enemy; the intolerant bigot or furious fanatic; the oppressive and unjust ruler; the harsh and rigid master; the sanguinary tyrant; the perfidious negotiator; the frivolous and capricious innovator; the mean and minute economist; the peddling trader and even the retail shop-keeper."* Lt. Moor on the contrary argues that "those, however, who do not choose to be carried away by the torrent of popular opinion, but, in preference to thinking by proxy, venture to think for themselves, can find the same excuse for the restlessness of Tippoo, as for that of any other ambitious sovereign; and on the subject of his cruelties, venture to express a doubt whether they may not possibly have been exaggerated." He ridicules the fantastic stories about Tipu's cowardice and suspicion which obtained credit and currency even among educated and intelligent Englishmen, and emphatically asserts that Tipu's subjects were as happy as those of

* *Select Letters of Tippoo Sultan*, p. x.

any other sovereign.* Major Dirom says that "his (Tipu's) country was found everywhere full of inhabitants, and apparently cultivated to the utmost extent of which the soil was capable; while the discipline and fidelity of his troops in the field, until their last overthrow, were testimonies equally strong, of the excellent regulations which existed in his army. His government, though strict and arbitrary, was the despotism of a politic and able sovereign, who nourishes, not oppresses, the subjects who are to be the means of his future aggrandisement, and his cruelties were, in general, inflicted only on those whom he considered as his enemies."† The English prisoners of Hyder gave Tipu credit for sympathy and generosity, but they had to change their opinion when he ceased to be the mere heir-apparent and became the autocratic sovereign of Mysore. Michaud, a Frenchman, could naturally be expected to be favourably inclined towards an ally of his king, and enthusiastically painted Tipu's regime as the most prosperous period in the history of his kingdom. Muhammadan writers like Husain Ali Kirmani had nothing but high-sounding encomiums to lavish upon their hero and applauded the qualities of his head and heart in fine phrases and ornate language. It is not, however, proposed to review here Tipu's career

* *A Narrative of the Operations of Captain Little's Detachment*, pp. 193-203.

† *A Narrative of the Campaign in India*, pp. 249-250.

or character in general, but our enquiry will be limited to his attitude towards Non-Muhammadans in general and Hindus in particular.

It has frequently been asserted that Tipu was a fanatic and a bigot, and failed to respect the religious susceptibilities of his Non-Muslim subjects. Hindus were forcibly converted and Christian Missionaries were expelled from his territories. Kirkpatrick opined that these wanton acts were not warranted by political needs, but suggests that "With regard......to his forcible conversion of so many thousands of the two latter tribes (Koorgs and Nairs) to the Mahommedan faith, he most probably thought such enormities no less warranted, both by the example and precepts of the founder of his religion."* Unfortunately the charge of forcible conversion cannot be lightly dismissed, supported as it is by unimpeachable evidence, furnished by the Sultan's own letters. Thus in a letter to Runmust Khan the Sultan writes: "We proceeded with the utmost speed, and, at once, made prisoners of forty thousand occasion-seeking and sedition-exciting Koorgs, who, alarmed at the approach of our victorious army, had slunk into woods, and concealed themselves in lofty mountains, inaccessible even to birds. Then carrying them away from their native country (the native place of sedition) we raised them to the honor of *Islâm*, and incorporat-

* *Select Letters of Tippoo Sultan*, p. xiv.

ed them with our *Ahmedy* corps."* This was not an isolated incident of its kind and we find references to other instances of forcible conversion both in the Sultan's own correspondence and in the narratives written by English prisoners. In a letter, dated the 13th February, 1756, to Budrûz Zumân Khan the Sultan approves of such forcible conversion in unambiguous language. "Your two letters, with the enclosed memorandums of the Nâimâ (or *Nair*) captives, have been received. You did right in causing a hundred and thirty-five of them to be circumcised, and in putting eleven of the youngest of these into the *Usud Ilhye* band (or class), and the remaining ninety-four into the *Ahmedy* troops, consigning the whole, at the same time, to the charge of the *Kiladâr* of *Nugr*."† In May of the same year the following order was sent to the Faujdar of Calicut—"Getting possession of the villain, Goorkul, and of his wife and children, you must forcibly make Musulmans of them, and then dispatch the whole under a guard to *Putn*."‡ The Malabar Christians were also converted in large number, as we learn from James Scurry, an English prisoner in Mysore and himself an unwilling convert (Scurry and a large number of English prisoners were circumcised by Hyder's order). "Their country was invested by Tipoo's army, and

* *Select Letters of Tippoo Sultan*, pp. 228-229.

† *Select Letters of Tippoo Sultan*, pp. 256-257.

‡ *Select Letters of Tippoo Sultan*, p. 310.

they were driven, men, women, and children, to the number of 30,000 to Seringapatam, where all who were fit to carry arms were circumcised, and formed into four battalions."* But for the discovery of fresh evidence, it might reasonably be concluded that Tipu seldom failed to add to the number of his Muslim subjects by forcible conversion and the Non-Muslim stood in daily fear of violent circumcision. A bundle of letters, discovered by Rao Bahadur K. Narsimhachar, throws fresh light upon the subject, and we find the Sultan in the totally unexpected roll of the protector of his Hindu subjects and patron of a Hindu monastery.

The village of Shringeri lies below a small hill on the left bank of the river Tungā. It derives its name from Sanskrit Shringagiri, or Rishyashringagiri, and, if tradition is to be credited, here lived in ancient times the great sage Vibhandaka and his greater son, Rishyashringa. The village is occasionally mentioned as Shringapura in some old inscriptions. In the eighth century the celebrated Hindu teacher Shankaracharya founded a *matha* or monastery at Shringeri with Sureshvara, a favourite disciple of his, as its head. The Swamis or Abbots of Shringeri, therefore, derive their spiritual authority from Shankara and claim to be his apostolic descendants. The monastery was enriched by rich donations from wealthy devotees and neighbouring princes, and the Jagadguru Shri

* A. W. Lawrence, *Captives of Tipu*, p. 197.

Shankaracharyya of Shringeri, as the Abbot is styled, commands the respect of millions of Hindus throughout India. In 1916 Mr. Narasimhachar discovered in this famous monastery a large number of letters addressed by Tipu Sultan on various occasions to His Holiness the Abbot. These letters are all couched in very respectful terms and implore the Swami to pray for the welfare of the kingdom.*

"Of Tipu's records at Shringeri," Rao Bahadur Narasimhachar informs us, "17 are dated in 1791 (Maulûdi or A.M. 1218-19); 5, in 1792 (A.M. 1219-1220); 2, in 1793 (A.M. 1220); 1, in 1794 (A.M. 1222); 1, in 1795; 1, in 1796 (A.M. 1224); and 2, in 1798 (A.M. 1225-26). Several of them refer to an attack on the country by three groups of enemies whose destruction the swami is requtsted to bring about by the performance of some religious ceremonies such as *śata-Chandi-japa* and *sahasra-Chandi-japa* and several more refer to the great loss sustained by the maṭha in consequence of a raid by the Mahrattas under Parashuram Bhau... ....From one of them, addressed to the svami, we learn that Mahratta horsemen raided Shringeri, killed and wounded many Brahmans and other people, pulled out the goddess Sharada and carried off everything found in the maṭha; that the svami, having therefore left Shringeri, was living

* *Annual Report of the Mysore Archæological Department for the year* 1916, pp. 10-11, and 73-76.

with four of his disciples at Karkala; and that on his writing to Tipu informing him of all this and telling him that without Government help in the shape of money and things it was not possible to re-consecrate the image of the goddess Sharada, the latter replied thus:—'People who have sinned against such a holy place are sure to suffer the consequences of their misdeeds at no distant date in this Kali age in accordance with the verse

Hasadbhih kriyate karma rudadbhir anubhuyate :

"people do evil deeds smiling but will suffer the consequences weeping." Treachery to gurus will undoubtedly result in the destruction of the line of descent. An order is enclosed to the asaf of Nagar directing him to give on behalf of Government 200 *rahati* in cash and 200 *rahati* worth of grain for the consecration of the goddess Sharada, and to supply other articles, if desired, for money. You may also get the necessary things from the *inâm* villages. Having thus consecrated the goddess and fed the Brahmans, please pray for the increase of our prosperity and the destruction of our enemies.' "

The language and the sentiments of this letter are such as might very well be attributed to a Hindu prince. Yet it was addressed by a Muhammadan ruler, commonly represented as an intolerant bigot, to a Hindu abbot who had suffered terribly at the hands of a Hindu army. The head of the Maratha state was a Brahman, the commander of the invading army was a Brahman, the Marathas displayed the ochre-coloured banner, the symbol of renunciation. Was it probable that a Hindu force commanded by a Brahman general in the service of a Brahman prince should desecrate the temple of Sharada, displace the image and despoil the apostolic descendant of the great Shankara of his worldly belongings, and horror of horrors, commit the unthinkable crime of Brahmanicide? The story is hard to believe, but it received corroboration from an unexpected quarter. On the 24th May, 1791, Trimbak Rao sent from the Maratha camp the following account of this deplorable incident to Bala Saheb of Miraj: " The army crossed the Tunga but the Lamans and the Pendharis had previously proceeded towards Shivmoghe. They went to the Swami's village of Shringeri and plundered it. They robbed the Swami of all his belongings, including the *danda* and *kamandalu* (ascetic's staff and water jug), and left nothing. Even women were molested and some of them sacrificed their lives, the images belonging to the Swami, consisting of those of gods and phalluses, were plundered. The Lamans brought away all the elephants and horses. The Swami fasted for five days and died (in consequence)."* When the news of these enormities reached Parashuram Bhau Patavardhan, the officer commadning the Maratha army, he had

* Khare, *Aitihasik Lekha Sangraha*, Vol. IX, p. 4506.

the miscreants arrested but nothing except the elephants could be recovered. The Swami of Shringeri started fasting in order to bring his grievances to the notice of the Maratha authorities, and afterwards wrote repeatedly to the Peshwa for the restoration of his property. Nana Fadnavis was anxious to appease the Swami's wrath, but it does not appear that the culprits were ever brought to book, nor do we know whether the aggrieved abbot received any compensation. Every Maratha leader had a number of professional plunderers with his army. They received no pay either from the state or from the general whose army they joined. They subsisted on what spoils they could take, and in lieu of the protection they received from the general, paid him a tax called *palpatti* or tent duty. The Shringeri temple was desecrated by the Lamans attached to the force of Raghunath Rao Kurundvadkar. In a letter, dated the 30th December of the same year, Raghunath Rao disclaimed all responsibility for the robbery and suggested that Lamans belonging to other detachments were guilty of the offence. He demanded an enquiry and the matter probably ended there.*

Thus we find that at least one important item in Tipu's letter is substantially corroborated by his enemies and we need not therefore question the accuracy of the other items. Tipu did indeed

* Khare, *Aitihasik Lekha-Sangraha,* Vol. IX, pp. 4557-58.

financially help the Hindu abbot to reinstal the image of the goddess Sharada, and this was not the only occasion when he assumed a friendly attitude towards the Swami of Shringeri. We are further told by Mr. Narasimhachar that " there are two records of Tippu, dated in the month of Khuradali (Ashvija) of the year Zabarjad (Virodhikritu), A.M. 1219 (1791). In one of them Tippu acknowledges receipt of the details of expenditure to be incurred for the ceremonies (*śata-Chandi-japa* and *sahasra-Chandi-japa*), expresses pleasure at the svâmi's decision to have *sahasra-Chandi-japa* performed for the welfare of the country and the destruction of the enemies, intimates that orders have been issued to the *âsaf* to supply everything that may be required and that the Amildar of Kophahôbali and Triyambakarâya, Mutsaddi of the Nagar *âsaf-kacheri*, have been directed to go to Shringeri, store up all the necessary things and supply them as required, and requests the svami to have the ceremony performed according to the prescribed rites, making money gifts to the Brahmans engaged and feeding 1,000 Brahmans every day."* In a subsequent letter the Sultan "expressed his pleasure at hearing that the ceremony of *sahasra-Chandi-japa* was commenced." Thus we see that Tipu not only tolerated Hinduism but actually went so far as to supply the Shri Shankaracharya of Shringeri

* *Annual Report of the Mysore Archæological Department for the year 1916*, p. 75.

with funds for reinstalling the displaced image in the Sharada temple and performing ceremonies like *sahasra-Chandi-japa.* It may be argued that Tipu was at this time hard-pressed by his enemies and wanted, therefore, to conciliate his Hindu subjects and at the same time to bring about the discomfiture of his enemies by means of these superstitious rites. But a zealous Muslim could not in any case sacrifice his principles by contributing funds for idol worship, and, however superstitious he might be, a bigoted Muhammadan could never believe in the efficacy of Hindu rites and religious ceremonies. We are, therefore, inevitably led to conclude that Tipu's bigotry and intolerance have been unduly exaggerated. Hyder and Tipu had been both brought up among Hindus in an atmosphere of religious tolerance, and, like most Indian Muslims, they believed, more or less, in the fundamental truth of all religions. Tipu was, therefore, quite sincere when he wrote to the Swami of Shringeri in 1793—"You are the *Jagadguru.* You are always performing penance in order that the whole world may prosper and the people may be happy. Please pray to God for the increase of our prosperity. In whatever country holy personages like yourself may reside, that country will flourish with good showers and crops."

How are we then to reconcile this indirect participation in Hindu rites with the forcible conversion of Tipu's Hindu subjects. The explanation is not difficult to find. Major Dirom was of opinion that "his (Tipu's) cruelties were in general, inflicted only on those whom he considered as his enemies." There is reason to believe that the honour of conversion was reserved only for those refractory Hindus upon whose unquestioning obedience the Sultan could not count. The loss of caste was and is regarded by the Hindus as the greatest disgrace, and the letters of Tipu hardly leave any doubt that he regarded conversion as an extreme form of punishment. He once warned the Koorgs that "if you ever again conduct yourselves traitorously or wickedly, I will not revile or molest a single individual among you, but making Ahmedies [*i.e., Musulmans*] of the whole of you, transplant you all from this country to some other."* This threat was literally carried out when the Koorgs again rose in rebellion. Nor was the Sultan inspired by any zeal for his religion when he suggested to Muhammad Beg Hamdani of Delhi that "all Musulmans should unite together; and considering the annihilation of infidels as a sacred duty, labour, to the utmost of their power, to accomplish that subject."† He was actually fighting against some Muhammadan rulers at that very moment, but he knew that a pan-Islamic programme was likely to appeal to the Musulman potentates in India and abroad.

* Kirkpatrick, *Select Letters of Tippoo Sultan*, p. 207.

† Kirkpatrick, *Select Letters of Tippoo Sultan*, p. 368.

Muhammad Beg, moreover, was hostile to the Marathas, the most inveterate enemies of the Mysore Chief. His ill-treatment of Roman Catholic clergymen was also due to political reasons and not to religious intolerance. The Padres were suspected of having assisted the English during the Second Mysore War.*

It is strange that Col. Wilks describes Hyder as " half a Hindoo " because he had ordered " the jebbum to be performed in the Hindoo temples." † But it is stranger that he should condemn Tipu as an intolerant bigot though he also believed in the efficacy of that ceremony. According to Wilks, " the tolerant spirit of Hyder, reconciled to his usurpation the members of every sect : appropriate talents regulated his choice of instruments, to the entire exclusion of religious preference.........A dark and intolerant bigotry excluded from Tippu's choice all but the true believers; and unlimited persecution united in detestation of his rule every Hindoo in his dominions. In the Hindoo no degree of merit was a passport to favor; in the Mussulman no crime could ensure displeasure." ‡ Tipu had, indeed, the misfortune of losing the

* Archivo Ultramarino, Lisbon, Officios dos Governadores, Maço, 14, No. 37.

† *Historical Sketches of the South of India* (2nd edition), Vol. I, p. 445.

‡ Wilks, *Historical Sketches of the South of India* (2nd edition), Vol. II, p. 382.

kingdom his father had founded, but it does not appear that he was less tolerant or more cruel than Hyder. The policy of wholesale transplantation and conversion of conquered people was initiated by Hyder. After the reduction of Chittledroog, Hyder had carried away 20,000 Bedars to the island of Seringapatam. "From the boys of a proper age, he formed the first regular military establishment of captive converts, in imitation of the Turkish Janissaries (new soldiers)."* Tipu simply followed in the footsteps of his far-famed father when he forcibly converted forty to fifty thousand unbelievers of Koorg and enlisted them in the Ahmedi corps. It was Hyder again, who introduced the practice of forcibly converting European prisoners,† and Tipu's treatment of these

* Wilks, *Historical Sketches of the South of India* (2nd edition), Vol. I, p. 407.

† A. W. Lawrence, *Captives of Tipu*, pp. 33-34. James Bristow writes: "In the month of September, 1781, about six months after my imprisonment, the Nyar, a Brahmin, and the commander of our guards, entered the prison early in the morning and selected Sergeant Dempster, with fifteen more of the prisoners, among whom were two young boys, drummers of the 73rd regiment; struck off their irons, and without deigning to utter a word, carried them away, for the purpose, as I soon after understood, of circumcising them. They resisted a long while, and bore very cruel treatment before they submitted to this operation, nor did they submit at last until they were stupefied with Majum, which they had been forced to swallow." Other prisoners, including Bristow, were sub-

unfortunate men was certainly not less humane than that of his father. The revenue officers of Tipu were mostly Hindus, and Hindus like Raja Ramchandra and Purnaiya enjoyed the Sultan's confidence and favour to the same degree as the most trusted Muhammadan minister of Mysore.* The Shringeri letters make it perfectly clear that Tipu knew how to placate Hindu opinion, and religious intolerance was not the real cause of his ruin.

jected to a similar treatment and incorporated in the Chela regiment.

* Wilks probably relied on the testimony of Husain Ali Kirmani, who observes:—" As the Sultan had a great aversion to Brahmans, Hindus and other tribes, he did not consider any but the people of Islam his friends, and therefore on all accounts his chief object was to promote and provide for them." *The History of the Reign of Tipu Sultan*, p. 230. The author probably wanted to secure the good opinion of Muslims for his hero.

———

PORTUGUESE RECORDS ON HYDER AND TIPU

The Portuguese had much to say about the two Muhammadan potentates under whom Mysore rose to so much power, and no student of this period can afford to ignore the huge mass of records preserved in the archives of Lisbon and Goa. Unfortunately these papers have hitherto received but inadequate attention, mainly because they are neither well kept nor easily accessible. It is, therefore, felt that a list of the letters bearing on Hyder and Tipu, included in the correspondence of the Portuguese Governors and Viceroys preserved in the Archivo Ultramarino of Lisbon, may be of some use to those who have no opportunity to examine them in original. The *officios dos governadores*, as these letters and correspondence are called, are kept in separate *maços* or packets. Unfortunately the labels on some of these packets are missing, and all the bundles cannot be readily traced. The following list is, therefore, necessarily incomplete. Reference has been given not only to the serial number of the packet but also to the serial number of the letters, and their respective dates have been, so far as possible, indicated. This will make it easier to secure transcripts of the relevant papers from Lisbon at a fairly reasonable cost. The Goa papers are preserved in bound volumes, but their condition is by no means satisfactory. Extracts from these records are being gradually published, and it may be hoped that papers relating to Hyder and Tipu will be available in print before long.

Maço II.

No. 12. 26 January, 1764 :—

A short biography of Hyder.

Maço III.

No. 44. 23 September, 1765 :—

An account of Hyder's navy.

No. 25. 12 December, 1765 :—

Another reference to the increase of Hyder's maritime power.

Maço IV.

No. 48. 3 February, 1770 :—

War with the Marathas.

Maço V.

No. 1. 24 February, 1778 :—

Hyder captures a Dutch fortress.

No. 61. 19 December, 1778 :—

Marquis Belcont, Governor of Pondichery, visited the western coast and went as far as Surat. The Portuguese suspected that his real object was to conclude an offensive and defensive alliance with Hyder Ali.

No. 63. 22 December, 1778 :—

An Austrian captain waited upon Hyder Ali and concluded a commercial agreement with him.

No. 66. 25 December, 1778 :—

Hyder took possession of the Maratha districts between the Krishna and the Ghats (near Phonda), and then marched towards the Tungabhadra. He afterwards proceeded against the Raja of Chittledrug.

No. 70. 28 December, 1778 :—

A brief account of Hyder's annexation of the Krishna-Tungabhadra *doab* and the slow progress of the projected harbour at Bhatkal.

Maço IX.

No. 26. 15 February, 1782 :—

Hyder still permits the Portuguese to trade with his ports.

Maço XII.

No. 18. 2 February, 1783 :—

Discusses the proposal of a treaty with Hyder and encloses letters from Sheikh Ayaz, Governor of Nagar.

N.B.—Hyder died in December, 1782.

No. 23. 10 February, 1783 :—

News about the second Mysore War and Hyder's death.

No. 55. 11 December, 1783 :—

Hyder's death and General Matthews' surrender to Tipu; terms of a draft treaty between Tipu and the English.

Enclosure :—A letter of M. Piveron de Morlas, French Charge de Affaires, dated the 17th October, 1783. The following lines from M. Morlas' pen deserve quotation.

" Since the death of Aidaralican things in this *darbar* are totally different. His successor possesses neither his spirit nor his great qualities, and it is said that he will not be able to retain long his great heritage. * * His *darbar* is wicked, ignorant, avaricious and false; and the actions of the prince are much resented."

Maço XIV.

No. 66. 26 March, 1784 :—

When Mangalore was captured by the English they took possession of the Portuguese factory there with all its artillery. Tipu recaptured the place and the Portuguese sought his permission for re-establishing their factory. But the Portuguese Vicar of the place was thrown into prison and the Christians were compelled to forsake their home and live at Seringapatam.

Maço XV.

No. 75. 6 May, 1784 :—

Enclosed a copy of the treaty between Tipu and the English.

No. 84. 9 May, 1784 :—

Tipu objected to Hayat Saheb's residence at Goa. He oppressed the Christians and compelled them to forsake their home. The Portuguese authorities apprehended that Tipu Sultan might invade Goa.

Maço XVI.

No. 35. 8 March, 1785 :—

Enclosure :—Letters to and from Tipu Sultan respecting his ill-treatment of Christians and imprisonment of their clergymen. Tipu complained that the Padres helped the English during the last war.

Maço XVII.

No. 69. 7 December, 1785 :—

An account of the reduction of Nargund and Kittur by the Mysore army.

Maço XVIII.

No. 3. 15 February, 1786 :—

Refers to Tipu's war against the Marathas and Nizam Ali.

No. 24. 12 April, 1786 :—

Rumour about Tipu's death not credited.

No. 30. 5 December, 1786 :—

Details of the war between Tipu and the Marathas.

Maço XX.

No. 86. 26 February, 1787.

Writes about Tipu's army. A French deserter informed the writer that Tipu's forces were very irregularly paid.

No. 95. 12 March, 1787 :—

A draft of a proposed alliance between the Portuguese and the Marathas against Tipu. (This draft has been published by Judice Biker in Vol. VIII of his *Tratados da India*).

No. 100. 20 July, 1787 :—

Conclusion of a treaty between Tipu and the Poona Government.

No. 103. 10 October, 1787 :—

Tipu reduced Kittur and declared that he would march to Belgaum next. The

Desais of the locality sought Portuguese assistance as the Poona Government proved lethargic.

Maço XXII.

No. 32. 18 February, 1788 :—

The only Portuguese factor, who was still in Tipu's country, was asked to write about the treatment he received from the Sultan. He complained that he was very badly treated. Among the new demands of the Sultan, he mentioned a present to the Governor at the beginning of each month, and another to be made whenever the Sultan received any good news.

Maço XXIII.

No. 20. 1 September, 1788 :—

Tipu's movements against the Marathas.

Maço XXIV.

No. 31. 14 March, 1789 :—

About Tipu and the Raja of Sunda.

No. 44. 10 March, 1789 :—

Tipu concluded a treaty of peace with the Marathas but it was violated by him soon afterwards.

Maço XXV.

No. 15. 23 February, 1790 :—

A general review of the political situation. Tipu's attack on the Travancore lines. One Kamaluddin is mentioned as the Superintendent of Tipu's fleet.

No. 17. 28 February, 1790 :—

The warm welcome that Tipu's envoys received at Paris led the Portuguese to suspect that Tipu and his French ally might have some designs against Goa.

No. 29. 4 March, 1790 :—

Further apprehension about Tipu's designs.

No. 30. 5 March, 1790 :—

A Frenchman went to Lisbon to buy arms, apparently for sale in Africa, but the Portuguese suspected that the arms were really meant for Tipu's use.

No. 44. 13 March, 1790 :—

Various rumours about war.

No. 55. 16 September, 1790 :—

The Triple Alliance and war against Tipu.

No. 58. 30 November, 1790 :—

A report of the campaign.

No. 60. 4 December, 1790 :—

A report of the campaign.

Maço XXVI.

No. 33. 18 April, 1791 :—

Maratha naval expedition against Tipu's coast.

Maço XXVII.

No. 20 :—

Progress of the allied armies.

No. 38. 19 April, 1791 :—

Retreat of General Meadows and operations of the Maratha fleet.

No. 47. 27 April, 1791 :—

Tipu closes his ports against the Portuguese.

Maço XXVIII.

No. 25. 20 April, 1792 :—

The war comes to an end. Hari Pant Fadke, the Maratha general, plays an important part in peace parleys. He is in constant correspondence with Tipu.

Maço XXIX.

No. 10. 20 February, 1793 :—

Tipu's ports are reopened to the Portuguese as a sign of amity.

No. 35. 10 March, 1795 :—

Tipu negotiates for restoration of Piro.

Maço XXXI.

No. 11. 22 February, 1797 :—

Rumours about Tipu's death. His inactivity during the succession troubles at Poona.

No. 37. 20 March, 1798 :—

A general account of the neighbouring princes of whom Tipu Sultan was one.

No. 39. 13 April, 1799 :—

A detailed survey of the political situation. Tipu's last war with the English.

No. 62. 12 September, 1799 :—

After Tipu's death some papers were discovered in his palace; these revealed a design against Goa in which the Sultan expected co-operation from Bonaparte.

Maço XXXII.

No. 70. 3 May, 1800 :—

A short narrative of Tipu Sultan's career.*

---

* It is needless to add that the above is a mere unannotated list of records, and no comment has been made about their accuracy.

APPAJI PANDIT, A FORGOTTEN MARATHA ADMIRAL

The Gaikwar once possessed a formidable fighting fleet and his men-of-war cruised about Surat and levied contributions on merchant vessels of all nationalities. About the middle of the eighteenth century, Appaji Pandit or Appaji Gopal, a daring sailor, commanded this fleet. He was dreaded by the English, the Dutch and the Portuguese alike, and his name found a place in the contemporary correspondence of all these three nations; yet such is the irony of fate that Appaji's exploits are quite unknown to-day to the average student of Maratha history. His name has been absolutely forgotten.

The first reference to the depredations committed by Appaji is found in the proceedings of a Bombay consultation, dated the 3rd of October, 1749. It says that, " Several depredations having been committed on the merchant Shybars to the northward, and an English merchant ship boarded by a Ketch, Grab and a number of Gallivats belonging to Appajee Pandit, who cruizes with those vessels about Surat Bar, it is agreed that the Commanders of the cruizers have orders to treat him as a public enemy and destroy his fleet, if possible, whenever they may happen to meet with it."*

* Bombay Public Consultations, Range, CCCXLI, No. 16.

From a letter, dated Batavia, the 20th August, 1751, it appears that the servants of the Dutch East India Company at Surat had made common cause with the English against "Appaya Pandit," whom they regarded as a pirate. This Appaya Pandit, it may be safely concluded, was the same person as Appaji Pandit of the Bombay Public Consultations. The Dutch were not pulling on well with the English at the time, and the commercial rivalry between the two nations embittered their relation. The Dutch authorities at Batavia, therefore, severely commented "on the imprudence of the servants in joining the English, who had repeatedly obstructed the Company, in an expedition against the pirate Appaya Pandit."* How this expedition ended we do not know, but we have reason to believe that the joint efforts of the English and the Dutch did not succeed in crushing Appaji, for in December, 1751, or in the first week of the next year, he boldly attacked near Surat a Portuguese fleet bound for Diu. In this action Appaji Gopal lost his life.

For a short narrative of the career and the last engagement of Appaji Gopal we are indebted to an interesting pamphlet by Francisco Raymundo de Moraes Pereira entitled *Annal Indico Lusitano dos successos mais memoraveis e das acçoens mais particulares do primeiro anno do felicissimo Governo do Illustrissimo, e Excellentissimo Senhor Francisco*

* *Press List of Ancient Dutch Records from 1657 to 1825* (Madras Records Department), p. 51, No. 519.

de Assis de Tavora Marquez de Tavora, published at Lisbon in 1753. Pereira says that "when a Portuguese fleet on its way from Daman to Diu arrived within sight of Surat, it was attacked by seven Gallivats supported by three Pals, belonging to Damaji Gaicavar, Commander-in-chief of Ituma Bay Dabaria (Uma Bai Dabhade) owner of the territories of Guzaratte. This pirate, full of vanity coupled with valour, had in the preceding year captured a boat carrying ivory from Diu to Surrate. He persuaded himself that he would have the same good fortune with the Pataxo, of which he had received certain information." The boat was attacked and the Marathas were almost on the point of boarding her, but they were ultimately beaten back. They fought boldly and did not leave before three hundred of them were killed, among whom was their admiral Appaji Gopal.*

Appaji, we learn from Pereira, received his early training in Angria's service. He then joined the Gaikwar's fleet and took many valuable prizes. He infested the neighbouring sea and earned great reputation with a huge fortune within a very short period. Even his enemies admired his courage and skill, and Pereira says that Appaji "lost his life gloriously." His wife, a worthy mate of the valiant sailor, performed the *sati*.† This is all that we know of Appaji Gopal. He who was the terror of

* Pereira, *Annal Indico Lusitano*, p. 77. The translation is not literal.

† Pereira, *Annal Indico Lusitano*, p. 79.

the European traders at Surat is remembered no more; so faithless is fame!

Who succeeded Appaji in his command, we do not know, but the Gaikwar fleet still continued to harass the merchant-men of Surat. In 1759, seven years after Appaji's death, the Government of Bombay sent William Andrew Price on an embassy to Poona. In a post-script to his instructions he was told, " As we expect you will meet Damaji at Poona, we would have you take an opportunity of intimating that we are willing to enter into an agreement with him that his vessels may no longer continue to annoy our trade, and if he makes any reasonable proposals, acquaint us therewith, but should he decline it, you are to declare to him that we shall take satisfaction for the depredations he has committed."* An amicable settlement was made, and Price wrote in his diary " Damaji sent me the orders I requested of him for the parganas or districts under his command paying the usual revenue to Surat Castle and for supporting the fleet; likewise an order to the commanding officer of his own fleet not to molest any vessels trading under the Hon'ble Company's protection."†

* Forrest, *Selections from Letters, Despatches and other State Papers preserved in the Bombay Secretariat*, Maratha Series, p. 128.

† Forrest, *Selections from Letters, Despatches and other State Papers preserved in the Bombay Secretariat*, Maratha Series, p. 137.

It may be noted that Appaji Gopal was not a pirate, though condemned as such by the trading companies of Europe. The rulers of the maritime districts of Western India claimed and often effectively exercised the sovereignty of the sea. They compelled alien vessels to buy their permit and seized and confiscated all ships unprovided with their passes. This practice was not confined to the indigenous powers alone. The English of Bombay, the Portuguese of Goa and the Dutch of Vingurla claimed the same privilege and derived no small profit from the sale of their passports. Appaji, as the commander of the Gujarat fleet, deemed it his duty to cruise along the coast and punish every foreign ship that might be found to sail without Damaji's pass.*

---

* For a fuller discussion of this question see Sen, *Military System of the Marathas*, Chapter XIII, pp. 241-257.

MARQUIS OF ALORNA'S INSTRUCTIONS TO HIS SUCCESSOR.

INTRODUCTION

The small districts forming the present province of Goa were not all annexed in the palmy days of the Portuguese empire. They are divided into two classes, the old and the new conquests. The former (*velhas conquistas*) consist of the island of Goa, the two provinces of Salsette* and Bardes with the district of Tiracol and the island of Angediva, while the latter (*novas conquistas*) include the rest of the province. In the history of the new conquests the Marquis of Alorna occupies a very high place.

Dom Pedro Miguel d'Almeida e Portugal, third Count of Assumar, first Marquis of Castello Novo, and afterwards Marquis of Alorna, had seen much service before he became Viceroy of Portuguese India in September, 1744. When he was appointed to this important office the outlook was far from bright. In 1739 Bassein surrendered to Chimnaji Appa and the Province of the North was annexed by the Marathas. The Maratha horse penetrated as far as Margão and threatened the safety of Goa. In 1740 the Sardesai of Kudal in-

* Should not be confused with Salsette near Bombay.

vaded Bardes, and Chaul was attacked by Tulaji Angria. The Portuguese realised their inability to defend this important port for any length of time, and were anxious to dispose of it by sale. They would prefer a European customer, but neither the Dutch nor the English could be induced to relieve them of their untenable possession. Chaul was at last sold to the Peshwa in September, 1740. In 1741 the Portuguese Government sent Dom Luiz de Menezes, Count of Ericeira and first Marquis of Louriçal, as Viceroy, for a second time, to retrieve their lost prestige in India. The Marquis of Louriçal had been accompanied by a strong force and he began his administration with vigour and resolution. He cleared the two provinces of Salsette and Bardes of hostile troops and captured the fortress of Ponda. But death cut short his victorious career and his immediate successors proved unequal to the difficult task with which they were confronted. The army was demoralised, the finances were in an unsatisfactory state and the Portuguese had no powerful ally in India. It was at this juncture that the Marquis of Castello Novo took charge of the government.

In a lengthy letter* Dom João V of Portugal elaborately explained the Indian situation to the new Viceroy, and enumerated the powers, Asiatic and European, friendly and hostile, with whom he would have to deal. The first and foremost among

* Biker, *Tratados da India*, Vol. VI, pp. 243-262.

them were the Marathas. They had inflicted a serious loss on the Portuguese by their conquest of Salsette and Bassein. Their fleet hampered Portuguese seaborne trade and their cavalry harassed the peaceful cultivators of Portuguese India. Dom João was by no means reconciled to the loss of the Province of the North, but he was constrained to acknowledge that the military resources of the Peshwa were incomparably superior to those of Portugal, and consequently, Dom Pedro Miguel d'Almeida was counselled to avoid fresh hostilities with him. The recovery of the lost provinces was to be always kept in view, but diplomacy and not armed contest was to be tried. The Viceroy could exploit the chronic dissension among the Maratha chiefs, and the death of Shahu, who had no son of his own, was expected to offer him an excellent opportunity for achieving his object.

With Persia the Viceroy was asked to cultivate friendly relations. The Portuguese State might find a useful ally in Tahmas Kuli Khan, better known as Nadir Shah. He might make a diversion in favour of the Portuguese, and the Marquis of Louriçal had already tried to renew the amity that once existed between Portugal and Persia. Nadir was anxious to establish his power on the sea. He had purchased some vessels at Surat and new men-of-war were being built for him. The King of Portugal had no doubt that the success of Nadir's naval policy would be of great benefit to the Portuguese, for, the Persian squadron would, no doubt, offer its protection to the merchant-men of Portuguese India.

The greatest injury to trade and commerce was caused by the fleets of the Angria, the Bhonsla, the Peshwa and the Raja of Kolhapur (Melondins). Of these the Angria was by far the most powerful. His fleet was daily growing more and more formidable, and his " piracy " not only injured trade and commerce in general but threatened Goa with starvation. Goa depended mainly on imported provisions but the sea was infested by Angria's ships, and the trading vessels were often intercepted. It was, therefore, of utmost importance that the squadron of Goa should always be kept ready for convoying merchant ships and bringing provisions.

Dom João was of opinion that the commercial interests of the State would be best served if the European nations made a common cause against the Angria and simultaneously attacked his strongholds. The Viceroy, however, would have to proceed with the greatest circumspection in his negotiations with the European trading companies. The Angria was indeed their common enemy, but they did not desire the prosperity of the Portuguese either. The English had often aggrandised themselves at the expense of the Portuguese, the French were engaged in contraband trade to the prejudice of Portugal, and the Dutch never lost any opportunity of exploiting the misfortunes of Goa.

The finances of the State also demanded the close attention of its new head. The loss of the

Province of the North naturally caused a fall in the revenue, but this was not met with a corresponding reduction in the old staff. This the Viceroy was strictly enjoined to effect. He was also expected to devise means for increasing revenue and reducing expenditure. During the last war with the Marathas, the nobility, the clergy and the commonalty of Goa had formed a *junta* and voted a new contribution of 10 p.c. This contribution was, however, stopped after a while, and the Marquis of Castello Novo was asked to revive the *junta* as well as the contribution. The Government monopoly of certain articles of trade was also expected to yield a good round sum and the Viceroy was asked to open some new industries at Goa. The cotton and silk industries of Thana were a source of great profit to the State, but the loss of that place had deprived the Portuguese of the income that they once derived from those industries. The King, therefore, advised his Viceroy to invite the artisans to settle at Goa where they should be encouraged to ply their trade to their mutual advantage.

Lastly the King commended the Christians of Malabar to the care of the Marquis. It had been reported that they were mercilessly persecuted by the Dutch Governor of Cochin. Many of the churches had been burnt and desecrated by the Dutch and the Bishop of Cochin found himself without a Cathedral. The Viceroy was urged to remedy their grievances as best as he could, as the

King had received repeated reports of their misery and persecution.

The Marquis of Castello Novo could not accomplish all that his master wanted, but he effectively restored the lost prestige of the Portuguese with their immediate neighbours. The Peshwa and the Angrias were indeed too powerful for him, Nadir's naval ambition was never realised, but the Sardesai of Kudal, otherwise called the Bhonsla, felt the weight of his arms before long. Early in 1746 the Viceroy invaded Bhonsla's territories and captured the strong fortress of Alorna. Alorna was situated on the banks of a big river, and the garrison was commanded by a near relative of the Sardesai, while the land force of Goa was led by a French officer, Colonel Pierripont. The fortress was reduced after five hours of hard fighting, and the victors in their fury committed many cruelties. Both the Viceroy and Monsieur Pierripont were highly rewarded by the Portuguese government for their services in this campaign. The Marquis attributed his success at Alorna to the use of petards with which the enemy was still unfamiliar. The fall of Alorna was succeeded by the evacuation of Bicholim. The King of Sunda was an irreconcilable enemy of the Bhonsla. The evacuated fortress was garrisoned by his troops at the invitation of the Viceroy. As the rainy season had already commenced and the Marquis was laid down with fever, he had to return to Goa without accomplishing anything further. But meanwhile, he had taken measures to induce the Desais of Sanquelim, Querim and Manerim and other influential chieftains of the locality to renounce their allegiance to the Sardesai of Kudal and to swear fealty to the King of Portugal. The campaign was re-opened in the autumn of the same year and the exertions of the Viceroy were rewarded with the reduction of Tiracol and Rarim. The last fortress to be captured was Neutim. After governing Portuguese India for six years with ability and distinction the Marquis of Alorna relinquished his office and was succeeded by Francisco de Assis de Tavora, fifth Count of S. João and third Marquis of Tavora. It was for his benefit that the retiring Viceroy wrote the brilliant *resumé* which follows. In this paper he enunciated the policy that ultimately led to the annexation of those districts which now form the new conquests. The Marquis of Tavora, however, did not possess the prowess and the statesmanlike qualities of his predecessor in office. His viceroyalty was not marked by any important event. On his return home he was accused of treason and beheaded.

PREFACE.

Your Excellency has been good enough to wish that I should give Your Excellency an idea of the public and private transactions of this Government so that Your Excellency may with the perspicacity of your intellect perceive much better from theory than I from six years' experience. I deem myself obliged to manifest my obedience, and lay bare my past errors for correction by Your Excellency, so that a solid structure without any defect of proportion may be built up from which will stream forth wisdom in the service of God and of the King, my master.

Two motives, equally powerful, make this work most agreeable to me. The first is a loyal and imperative obedience to the mandate of His Most Faithful Majesty ordering all who hold office to advise their successors. As to the second, it might look like insincerity to use the strongest language, but favourably received, my words cannot offend even the most delicate ears, and shall serve as a visible demonstration of the ties that closely bind me to Your Excellency, and effectively contribute to improve that fidelity. I can, therefore, freely publish the close friendship that at all time without fail I shall profess to Your Excellency and, if Divine Providence permits, shall bind us ever with indissoluble ties.

[8] For me it is the strongest inducement, and the richest pledge Your Excellency can receive is the assurance that I am truly much interested in the glory of Your Excellency's name; and if it is possible for men to look into the secret of human hearts, Your Excellency will then see in mine, that between your and my hopes, between your and my happiness, I cannot give preference to either but consider both as one indivisible entity.

To avoid confusion and to make this discourse easily intelligible to Your Excellency, I shall divide it in three parts. In the first part I shall deal with the petty princes and potentates, our neighbours, who have dependencies near this State, beginning with friends to pass afterwards to the enemies; and I shall here give information also about their mode of war, and the measures I adopted to defend myself from them. The second part treats of the nations of Europe and the relation we have with them, and the third deals with the domestic Government and the internal affairs of this State.

FIRST PART.

[9] The King of Canara* is the most rich and powerful (chief) on this coast. Tht rice trade, that supports the whole of Malabar and [10] some

* Otherwise known as the King of Bednur. The dynasty derives its names from Keladi, the native village of its founder, and also from Ikeri, the second capital of the Nayaks. " Their ancestors, according to the *Keladi Raya Paditti*, their family chronicle, had originally been heredi-

parts of Muscat, richly contributes the vast wealth to his country, which this King hoards and is thereby made the richest of his class. In his district we

tary *gowdas*, or chief of five or six villages in the neighbourhood of Keladi." (Heras, *The Aravidu Dynasty of Vijayanagara*, Vol. I, p. 177.) Chauda, the founder of the Keladi or Ikeri dynasty, discovered some buried treasure while ploughing his land, hired a number of mercenaries, and subsequently obtained from the King of Vijayanagara a formal grant for the district he had seized. His son Sadasiva earned fresh honours and rose to eminence in the Vijayanagara service. The descendants of Sadasiva removed their capital to Ikeri, where Pietro della Vale visited the ruling chief Venkatappa Nayak in 1623. The Nayaks of Ikeri assumed independence after the decline of Vijayanagara power. Shivappa Nayak, the most well known ruler of this line and a contemporary of Shivaji, removed his capital to Bednur or Bidururu, the town of bamboos. The last King of Bednur was Baswappa Nayak who died in 1755. Eight years later the kingdom was conquered by Hyder Ali from Baswappa's widow. (Bowring, *Haider Ali and Tipu Sultan*, pp. 35-39.) In 1631 a treaty was concluded between Virappa Nayak, King of Canara, and Conde de Linhares, Viceroy of Portuguese India (Biker, *Tratados da India*, Vol. I, pp. 370-273). By this treaty the port of Honawar or Onore was opened to the Portuguese and they obtained the right of cutting timbers in any part of the kingdom without paying any dues or customs, and of purchasing pepper freely whenever they may need it. They also obtained a specified quantity of rice. In 1671 they were permitted to open their factories at Barcelore, Mangalore and Honawar. Seven years later the King of Bednur gave the Portuguese land and materials for building factories at various places under his jurisdiction.

have a factory at Mangalore* with various advantages and privileges over other nations, for provisioning of this State, as Your Excellency can find in the treaties of [11] peace that are in the Secretariat. We have lived for a long time in peace and (on terms of) good relation with this King, and it is of the utmost importance that this relation should be kept inviolate, since we are dependent on it for our food-stuff in this country which does not produce (crops sufficient to supply) food for more than four months in the year.

[12] It seems incompatible with what I have said above of this Prince being very powerful, but it is also a fact that the wealth he possesses does not serve any other purpose than that of hoarding and is not of any use to him. He does not permit forts to be built in his country, so that in case of hostile invasion, the enemy may not establish themselves therein. [13] He has no troops, or they are so few, that the expense he incurs for them is very small. During the last two years Angria led two expeditions to Mangalore and Honore,† sacking these two ports from where he retired with the most valuable spoil. To prevent a third invasion he (the King of Canara) ultimately sent me a proposal that he had decided to form an armada and begged that I should let this fleet unite

* Mangalore is an important seaport and chief town of the South Kanara District of Madras.

† Honavar is a seaport, fifty miles south-east of Karwar.

with ours, suggesting that it would obey the orders of our Captains, for he has none of ability, and that both the fleets should cruise from Melondim* to his coast and attack Angria when necessary. To all this I responded in the affirmative, in a state of almost infallible certainty that such an armada would never be made, and I excused myself from this undertaking begging him (to fulfil) certain fundamental conditions of the treaty of peace concluded with him by Senhor Viceroy D. Rodrigo da Costa.† But he never fulfilled this treaty and my answer to this King Your Excellency will find in the books of the Secretariat.‡

[14] The Zamorin§ was in ancient times the most powerful king on the Malabar coast and the greatest enemy the Portuguese had. Now he is found reduced (in power) and almost dominated by the Moors living in his country, whom this Prince

* Malwan, chief town of a sub-division of the same name in the Ratnagiri District of Bombay. Here Shivaji built the famous naval stronghold of Sindhudurga. Malwan was under the jurisdiction of the Raja of Kolhapur, who ceded it to the British in 1812. The Malwan pirates caused troubles till the first decade of the last century.

† Dom Rodrigo da Costa was Viceroy of India from 1707 to 1712.

‡ The reference is probably to Livros dos Reis Visinhos.

§ The Zamorin was one of the few Indian princes with whom the Portuguese had to deal after their arrival in India. His kingdom was reduced and annexed by Hyder Ali of Mysore.

tolerates, so that he may not lose the trade, which they bring to his ports. In the port of Calicut* we have a factory that in the time of Senhor Marquis de Louriçal† was united [15] to the Vicarage of that parish. The same King pays (a contribution) to our Factor and this serves to procure wood, cocoanut fibres,‡ whale oil, plaster and ammunition for Ribeira, which is carried in our frigates and sent to that port.

The Nabobs of Kittur and of Saonoor,§ (whose states are) situated above the Ghats, are

* An ancient town in Malabar District of Madras. The Zamorin of Calicut was not a friend of the Portuguese and did not permit them to build a factory in his city. On several occasions the Portuguese made serious efforts to capture Calicut, but without any success. The town was taken in 1765 by Hyder Ali.

† Dom Luiz de Menezes, Conde de Ericeira, afterwards first Marquis of Louriçal, was Viceroy of Portuguese India from 1717 to 1720, and again from 1741 to 1742.

‡ Cairo, literally fibres from the outermost shell of Cocoanut.

§ The founder of the principality of Savanur was Abdul Rauf Khan, a Pathan officer of Bijapur. The principality was considered to be subordinate to the Nizam of Hyderabad. The Nawab, though connected by marriage with Tipu Sultan, made an alliance with the Peshwa. The Nawabs of Savanur are descendants of Abdul Karim Bahlole Khan, the famous Bijapur minister and adversary of Shivaji. Savanur is now a feudatory state in Dharwar District of Bombay. (*Gazetteer of the Bombay Presidency*, Vol. XXII, pp. 792-804.) The Chief of Kittur was a Hindu with the title of Desai.

under the Moghul King, and have little dealings with us, but none the less we live in friendship and good relationship with them and can safely look upon them as friends.

[16] The Sunda King* is a weak and unwarlike prince who has inherited from his father his

* The King of Sunda was originally a feudatory of the Raja of Vijayanagara. It is said that the founder of the family married a princess of the imperial house of Vijayanagara and was on that occasion elevated to the rank of a King. The principality was reduced and annexed by Hyder Ali in 1763. The King then took refuge with the Portuguese of Goa. In 1790 the deposed King of Sunda tried to recover his lost principality by concluding an alliance with the Marathas. But the Portuguese apprehended that an alliance of the Sunda Raja with the Marathas or the English would threaten the security of Goa. " A treaty was hurriedly entered into between the Portuguese and the King of Sunda, dated the 17th January, 1791, in which the latter abdicated, and assigned to the Portuguese all his rights in the territories of Ponda, Zambolim and Panchamal, together with their several dependencies, as well as the fortress of Cabo de Rama, and the jurisdiction of Canacona. The King of Sunda further agreed to make certain money allowances for the support of a Portuguese garrison at Piro. In two secret articles that were attached to the treaty, the king of Sunda further pledged himself not to leave Goa, and to endeavour to recover from the Mahrattas his former territories of Ponda, Zambolim, Supem, and others that were now held by them." (Danvers, *Portuguese in India*, Vol. II, pp. 448-49.) The descendant of the King of Sunda now lives in Portuguese India and is treated with great respect and honour.

kingdom, timidity and vices, specially addiction to drinking. [17] All who have any business with him must be prepared for a purgatory of patience, such is his dilatoriness and indolence even in matters demanding great promptitude. An example will show better than I can speak of. I knew that the Marathas intended to take possession of some strongholds very near to this State. I at once sent him information so that it might be anticipated and he might be on his guard. This, which would have moved any other sovereign to action, was for him a matter of great indifference. After [18] some months Shahu Raja, the supreme ruler of the Marathas, died; this prevented his ruin, and after one year and several months his lethargy permitted him to answer my letter, a few days before Your Excellency arrived at this port. Hence Your Excellency can infer whether this Prince is good for a neighbour, as he does not disturb this State. He is not of any use as a friend either, since he does not take interest in any thing except his own pastimes. In spite of all this, and though his troops and his people are a timid and cowardly race on whose constancy no reliance can be placed, many reasons lead us to maintain good relations with this Prince; first, for his being the nearest neighbour, secondly, [19] because from his lands we receive the better pepper as cargo for the homebound ships, enough wood for small vessels, some rice and many necessary food-stuffs; thirdly because a large number of Desais, vassals of this

State, have lands, which constitute their Desaidoms, in the province of Ponda, which is in the near neighbourhood of our country; fourthly, because in the same respect we undergo a sort of subordination in various cases (to him), not indeed by law but by ancient custom; fifthly, because during the invasions of the Marathas, the Ghats, over which [20]they usually come, are in his dominions, and we occupy them with his and our sepoys, which we would not be able to do, should there be any objection from his side; [21] the enemy would enter through the province of Salsette without any opposition; while we require his troops, he cannot hesitate to help us. Granting his troops are few and timid, these in any case add to the number of others and increase their bulk, which is of great value, when an Asiatic enemy is concerned.

Before we pass on, Your Excellency must be told that from information I had from different quarters I learnt that the English actually have an emissary of theirs at Sundem, the residence of the King of Sunda, from whom they solicit an agreement to sell them for a fixed price all the pepper that his country produces, and they also beg his permission to let them establish themselves anew at Carwar, whence [22] the Sundans drove them years ago. I also know that Nana* has another emissary in the same court to beg permission that the vessels of his fleet may always freely enter the Sunda ports

* Peshwa Balaji Baji Rao.

whenever it should be necessary for them. Either of these negotiations is of great importance and peril to this State. If the English prevail upon Sunda to contract for all the pepper, there will not be any place (from where) to buy it for the cargo of (our) home-bound ships, and if they establish themselves for the second time at Karwar, they will easily deprive us of this commodity, the only one we have to-day in which to employ the capital that merchants remit from home. Karwar is from Goa a little more than twelve leagues and will be (a) certain and inevitable (refuge) for our deserters. Your Excellency saw and examined the letter that I lately wrote to the King of Sunda upon this subject, reminding him of the peace* that he concluded with the Senhor Marquis de Louriçal, in which he undertook not to concede an establishment to any (other) European nation in the district of Karwar or in any other part of his dominions. I think that Your Excellency should make all the endeavour to obstruct this negotiation of the English, and to prevent (their) establishment at Karwar, as well as (their) contract for pepper, offering to conclude with the Raja a (fresh) treaty by which this State will undertake to take from him annually one thousand or fifteen hundred *Khandis* of pepper, which is the normal crop of a year. It is probable that the Sunda, having assurance about the export and sale of all his pepper, the

* The text of the treaty has been published by Judice Biker in his *Tratados da India*, Vol. VI, pp. 239-243.

payment being so safe in the hands of this State, [23] may agree to the said settlement, and the easiest way to prevail on him is to bribe his ministers liberally.

Some theorists may tell Your Excellency that the King of Sunda did not ratify the abovementioned treaty of peace; for they imagine that the Asiatic nations observe among them the same reasonable formalities of law as the nations of Europe. I say this treaty is in force, for, the Sunda has respected certain clauses of it; to wit, all that touch the missionaries and our religion; he has paid forty thousand Xerafins with which he promised to compensate us; I ordered the demolition of the stalls of Talavarda* near Coculim with which he complied, I caused restitution of the small vessels that we detained at Piro; and I always strove for the observance of all the clauses of this peace, which may be found subscribed by Calapaya and Custam Rao, plenipotentiaries of the Sunda Raja. The suggestion that the treaty does not subsist for want of ratification is of a fantastic foundation, so to say. I have finished with the friends, and shall now pass to the enemies.

The Angrias, who are the scourge of this coast from the point of [24] Diu to Calicut, (had their origin) came into prominence shortly before the ad-

* One of the three villages ceded by the King of Sunda by the treaty of 1742. The Portuguese took possession of these villages in 1755 and they were included in the province of Salsette.

ministration of Senhor Viceroy Caetano de Mello e Castro,* and by their piracies rose to such power that to-day they are dreaded and respected by all. These two brothers† (have) divided their dominion in two parts; the first, called Talagy Angria, has made his headquarters at Guiriem,‡ he is the nearest neighbour to Goa, and is very powerful. The second, called Managy Angria, has established himself at Culabo§ near Bombaim. The latter, (who) is near [25] the Province of the North, has his dominions encircled by the possessions of Nana, and has always solicited our friendship and desired anxiously that we should recover that province, so that he may have in us a better neighbour than the Marathas, from whom he has received continuous insults. Since I arrived here, there was not a single occasion when he did not offer me his maritime forces for some enterprise, principally against Nana. I never gave him a positive reply nor omitted to

* Caetano de Mello e Castro was Viceroy from 1703 to 1707.

† It is not known for certain whether Tulaji and Manaji Angria were full brothers or step-brothers.

MATHURA BAI = KANHOJI ANGRIA = GAHINA BAI

Sakhoji Sambhaji (sons of Mathura Bai)

Tulaji Manaji Yesaji Dhondji (sons of Gahina Bai)

‡ Gheria, better known as Vijayadurg in the Devgad Sub-Division of Ratnagiri District. In 1756 Gheria was reduced by Clive and Watson in co-operation with a Maratha force.

§ Kolaba.

thank him for his good wishes and I have been keeping up friendly correspondence with him. I did not (venture to) enter into negotiations with him, for I happened to know that he is always drunk and does not know (how) to read and write. All his negotiations are made through his Brahmans who dominate and hoodwink him, for he cannot by himself examine or decide them, and any negotiation, had it been proposed to him, would be known to Nana through these very Brahmans. In these circumstances I do not know under which class, that of friends or that of enemy, to place this chieftain, but it is safest to count him a neutral so long as his difference with Nana endures.

During the last four years Talagy Angria has proposed peace on several occasions at different times. Witnessing the fair success that Divine Providence gave us against the [26] Bounsulo, he proposed to me that we should both unite to attack the [27] common enemy. I replied that if through God's favour we had obtained what we wanted without his help, we needed it much less now. When the French squadron came to winter in this port, he feared that we might come against Guiriem in alliance with the French and persistently repeated the same proposal and further extended it so that he not only solicited peace with us but also wanted that I should act as a mediator for the treaty that he contemplated with the French. From this I perceived that in this proposal it was fear that prompted him rather than good will.

When reinforcement arrived in 1748, supposing it of greater strength than it (actually) was, he urged me anew for an alliance, soliciting from me help for a joint attack on the fortress of Monsurem,* which the Bounsulo had taken from him by surprise shortly before. Moreover he asked me to sell him the fortress of Neutim and the Carlim river† which I had recently conquered. This proposal I promptly rejected on various pretexts, for, it is ten leagues from the bar of Goa, and because the neighbourhood of Angria would be more perilous than that of the Bounsulo. I listened to his other proposals, being certain that they would have no effect. I replied that [28] as the expedition would be to his interest only and not to ours, he must pay the expenses of the fleet and munitions. He generously said he was ready to meet all the costs and enquired about the amount in order to remit it. I asked of him two hundred thousand rupees, to which he replied that he would at once put himself in the field in order to march, that I should send the reinforcement, adding that what touched the payment of expenses between friends could be adjusted after the action, which signified well that he meant to say that he would pay nothing, and as I perceived this, I kept him engaged in this negotiation, without accepting or rejecting (his offer). In the meantime he paid our vessels some

* Masura, near Malwan.

† The river Karli which falls into the sea near Malwan. Nivti fort, six and half miles south of Malwan.

attention. His envoy is actually waiting here for our answer and the final conclusion (of the treaty). Your Excellency will find the proposal for peace he made in the Secretariat, and whatever it may be, Your Excellency may be sure that it will not have more duration, firmness and subsistence than suits the interest of this chieftain, and that whatever may be the promises and oaths of treaty, there is no faith nor law that predominates his convenience. Under this principle it will suit us very much to protract the negotiation skilfully or conclude with him a treaty of reciprocity which may not bind us to anything (definite), for though no other benefit may come out of it than his not seizing our ships, it will suffice for his not hampering our commerce.

The reigning family of the Marathas is divided into two branches.* The first is that of Shahu Raja, supreme ruler of the Marathas, who has his court at Satara; and the other is that of Sambhaji Raja, first cousin of the former, who has his court at [29] Kolhapur. These two cousins divide their dominions by an imaginary line. Shahu Raja, taking advantage of the decline of the Moghul Empire and the infidelity of the Generals of the

```
*SAI BAI    =    SHIVAJI        =     SOYRA BAI
         |                  |
     Sambhaji   Tara Bai=Rajaram=Rajas Bai
         |              |         |
      Shahu          Shivaji III Sambhaji II
         |              |
     Adopted   =    Ran, Raja
```

Emperor, overruns and ravages with the army of his Captains the whole of the extensive territory from the kingdom of Cambay to Bengal, making all the provinces through which it passes tributary to him after devastating and robbing and depriving them of their incredible wealth. The district of Sambhaji Raja extends from that of Talagy Angria to the extreme confines of Canara, and it is supposed that the whole of Conkan, from the foot of the Ghats, is tributary to him. In it are included the territories of even the Angria and the Bounsulo, it is also supposed that the whole of the district of Goa is tributary to him. To this we never agree, nor do we pay him any tribute. The kings of Sunda and Canara pay him considerable tribute.

The system of Maratha Government is different from that of all others, and in truth, the sovereign is a kind of phantom or idol whom his subjects adore so long as they like. Shahu Raja, the supreme Prince, arrogates to himself the prerogative of issuing orders in the territories, of which he imagines himself the master, as well as in those of his cousin Sambhaji Raja, but his orders are seldom, if ever, executed. His council is composed of four or five principal ministers, [30] each one of whom has (distinct) authority and separate armies. The most powerful among them is Nana, son of Baji Rao who conquered from us the Province of the North, and can effectively bring into the field an army of fifty thousand horse, maintained at his cost. He possesses immense treasures.

For going on an expedition with the armies the permission of the ruler of Satara is solicited, and he indicates the regions where they are to go on their raids. The permit is not obtained without a sum of several lakhs of rupees which is paid or promised before setting out. The permission obtained, the leader of the troops gets a tacit or express *carte blanche,* to perpetrate all imaginable extortions and atrocities without any dependence upon or subordination to anybody. The hardship caused by fighting is not so much (distressing) as the damage done, and it is caused more through the terror and panic of the people than by the sharp edge of the sword and battles. Where they find nothing to plunder and meet only with resistance, mainly from fire, they engage themselves no more. It does not seem that the conquest of the Province of the North was an exception to this, for in that enterprise they gained much and risked little, as the loss of twenty thousand men, that they suffered in the siege of Bassein, was of no moment to them, nor was it equivalent to the huge sum [31] that the province yields them to-day. Shahu Raja has so few troops of his own that they are just sufficient for his guard only. Thus his is a precarious power, (maintained) more by the forces of his ministers than by his own.

Shahu Raja died last year. Nana, powerful as he was, could ascend the throne, but being a Brahman, his caste stood in his way as he was excluded from this high prerogative according to the rules of his caste.* Still he wanted to set up as sovereign one devoted to him, who would be his subordinate so that he might make himself independent with absolute dominion over all, leaving to (the puppet king) only the semblance of majesty. This caused great bitterness in the heart of the Marathas who neither tolerated nor approved (of the idea) that the Brahmans, their servants, should be their masters. It was easy for Nana to find out an unknown person, false or real, alleging him to be of the same family and blood as Shahu.† But

* Though Brahmans are excluded from the throne by the rules laid down by the ancient Shastras, many Brahmans did actually become Kings and this obsolete rule would by no means prove an insuperable obstacle to the Peshwa.

† After Shahu's death his widow adopted Ramraja, a grandson of Rajaram. (See Note, p. 206.) Soon after his appointment to the Peshwaship, Balaji Baji Rao, *alias* Nana, had indeed entered into a secret agreement with Sambhaji of Kolhapur to effect a union of the two crowns of Satara and Kolhapur after Shahu's death. But Shahu bitterly hated Sambhaji and would not hear of his crown passing to his cousin of Kolhapur. Tara Bai, Sambhaji's step-mother, gave out that her grandson was alive, and Balaji Baji Rao came to an understanding with her. But the veracity of Tara Bai was strongly suspected and she had to eat from the same plate as Ramraja before some of the most suspicious grandees could be induced to admit that Ramraja was a genuine descendant of the great Shivaji. Tara Bai, however, subsequently repudiated her solemn statement and no definite conclusion about Ramraja's origin is therefore possible. It is quite likely that her later repudiation was

many, or almost all, persuaded themselves that the contrary was the case, and entertained a more likely suspicion that he was a humble man of low origin. Nana's power, however, prevailed, and he placed on the throne a puppet whose figure and countenance almost confirmed his base origin. All yielded to force and to the fear of punishment, but it caused such commotion in the hearts of the grandees that jealousies and controversies on this subject endure even now, and it is of the utmost importance to this State that these should continue [32] and that these people should be in their heart disunited, so that Your Excellency may not experience in his first year that disquiet which this enemy is in the habit of causing, and may have time to know the Marathas and the people of this land.

Sambhaji Raja, of the second branch of the Maratha royal house, to whom by the right of blood belonged the crown and succession of his cousin Shahu Raja, intended to go to Satara, when that prince (Shahu Raja) was on the verge of death, to assert at the same time his claim. Nana, who was prepared to pitch himself against all who were opposed to his scheme, had encamped at Satara a corps of twenty thousand horse during the illness of Shahu, and as soon as he learnt of the resolution of Sambhaji, ordered all the roads and by-paths to be held by the troops, with instructions to prevent

really meant to put the Peshwa in the wrong. But it is equally possible that she foisted a supposititious child on the credulous people of Maharashtra to serve her political ends.

all who wanted to enter the capital without his consent. This he did, not because he had any fear of a weak and untalented prince (like Sambhaji), but to prevent (his arrival) from serving as a pretext to the malcontents who wanted tumultuously to set him up as king, asserting the incontestable right that he had to the crown. As soon as Sambhaji arrived near Satara, Nana sent word to him that his cousin was dead, and if perchance this visit was meant to bid him farewell, it had already become useless, and he might therefore return to Kolhapur. Sambhaji did so, yielding to Nana's power, and it can be imagined well what hatred he will feel for him, as his wife,* who entirely dominates him, is by nature so industrious and cunning and by temper so bad that in order to achieve her object she spares neither industry nor diplomacy nor the diabolic art.

I mentioned above the Bhonsla's dependence on Sambhaji Raja, and on this pretext the latter wanted to constitute himself a mediator for a peace between this State and that chieftain. He wrote to me that as the District of the Dessais of Kudal was under his dominion, I should entrust to him the strongholds I had conquered from the Dessais or direct his flag to be hoisted on them, and that we might

* Jija Bai of Kolhapur was a masterful lady. That she was cunning cannot be denied, particularly as she substituted a male child for a posthumous daughter of her husband (by another wife). The intrigue, however, was discovered, but she forced the Peshwa to acknowledge her right to adopt a son.

afterwards come to a settlement of the matter. I replied that I had been so long [33] waging war to chastise the Bhonsla, without in the space of three years this extravagant idea having occurred to him; I had obtained by force of arms the strongholds he mentioned, and I did not count on restoring them to him or allowing any flag, other than that of the King, my master, to be hoisted before defending it to the last. It was easily perceived how fictitious his pretensions were, for in the preceding year Sambhaji Raja had begged me to help him against the Angria, promising to assist me afterwards with all his forces to expel the Bhonsla totally from his country and to divide the conquered territories between us, and that it ill agreed with the proposals he now made. With this prince we have a treaty of peace, as ill observed as several others we concluded with other Hindu chieftains. After war had been declared against the Bhonsla, he sheltered some Gallivats that were in the port of Melondim and cruised in alliance with the Gallivats of that stronghold, commanded by Hiroji Naik, and harassed the Parangues that came to Goa with provision, and when satisfaction was demanded for this infringement of peace he replied that it had been done by the Bhonsla. Hiroji Naik, when interrogated about it, said that he was a subject of Sambhaji Raja.

While at Neutim, I did not lack the desire of turning my arms against the stronghold of Melondim, which is one league from the former place, for it is the most important place for the security of this coast, as it is an island, separated by a narrow canal from the main land, where all vessels, large and small, can gather. It juts out into the sea in the shape of a cape, and serves as a point for the navigators from the North to the South. The stronghold is of an extensive circuit, but so far as we could judge from that distance, it is of little strength, for it has no trench, and at that time it had (a) small garrison; but the month of December was far advanced and it was time to fit the home-bound fleet, and I could not delay. This enterprise was, therefore, postponed for a better occasion, or, perhaps, because the Divine Providence wills that this will be the first conquest which Your Excellency may grace with your presence and may accomplish by your [34] martial valour. Before Your Excellency attempts it, it will be necessary (to send) to explore the weakest part whence it can be attacked and where it will be most convenient to disembark. All depend on good scouts and a strict secrecy. Should they be heathens or the natives of the land, Your Excellency should neither trust their information, nor expect (them) to keep the secret, as on so many occasions we had experienced when we entrusted them with similar affairs, but you should find out some pretext and secretly send some intelligent engineers to bring more reliable news. When Your Excellency obtains possession of it, as I expect (you will), Your Excellency will consider whether it will be proper to demolish Neutim, for it is a place of little importance and very risky, as there is no water within the stronghold, and there is no bay, nor any port where the smaller vessels can be received, and its coast is much exposed in the summer to the North-east and in the winter to the South, and the South-east wind causes such high waves that for many days it becomes impossible to land. Moreover the garrison there will suffer many inconveniences.

I do not think that the injury that we shall thus cause Sambhaji Raja can be of great prejudice to us, nor (is it likely that) Nana, though more powerful, will help him; perhaps before he cares to find himself embroiled with us, we shall reduce his district, so that busy in defending himself, he may forget to disturb Nana with his plans. The Angria, having rebelled against him, can hardly be expected to help him. The only one who can give him some assistance is the Bhonsla, but his troops are so few that we need not fear them. I conceive this conquest to be of the utmost importance to this State, because with it we shall be in possession of the ports of Melondim, Rarim,* Arandem,† Chapora,‡

* Redi or Yashvantgad in the Ratnagiri District of Bombay and not far off from Vengurla. For a description of the fort see *Bombay Gazetteer*, Vol. XXII, pp. 369-371.

† The Araunda or Terekhol river forms the Southern boundary of the Ratnagiri District. The fort of Terekhol is about six leagues from Pangim and forms the northern limit of the Portuguese province of Goa.

‡ Chapora is about two leagues from Goa, the Sal, otherwise called the Betul, is 9½ leagues from Goa.

Goa, [35] the river Sal as far as Angediva, without leaving to the pirates any place where they can gather their vessels. Beyond Melondim [36] the sea opens to the north and to the south; we shall be able to run promptly with our ships against all our enemies when they are discovered, we shall more securely control the river Carlim, and the enemy will not be able to build or gather in it any of his ships, we being owners of both the banks.

The Dessais of Kudal, otherwise called the Savanta Bhonslas, are those who have now open war with us. As Your Excellency has been well informed of the movements that obliged me to declare war and what has followed since, I excuse myself from dilating upon this matter: The profit we have hitherto derived is the reputation of our arms among the Asiatic nations, and that this bad neighbour has been reduced to extreme submissiveness, rendering us more respected than we were when I arrived here. The most solid (result) that can be obtained will be after the peace, provided it is becoming of the State; meanwhile it is not a small benefit that we receive in reducing the income and the strength of the enemy. Though we do not profit by the produce of the lands we have conquered from him, because the cultivators run away and forsake the villages, we are causing the enemy the loss of a revenue of one hundred and as many thosuand rupees, or so, for more than four years.

On various occasions this enemy has proposed peace to me, either directly through his emissaries, or indirectly through Nana or through Sambhaji Raja, who protects him; but always with vague conditions and clauses for restoring to him the conquered lands and strongholds, which Your Excellency will be able to see and examine in the books of the Secretariat. I have been always ready to listen to any proposal (of peace), but as it did not stipulate for any definite term and was hardly honourable to the State, it did not seem to me right to continue the negotiation or waste time uselessly. If we restored to him all that we have seized by force, he would return to his old and usual insolence and we would see ourselves immediately obliged to begin his chastisement anew; and so long as I had in my power the prize and trod his country as my own, the attempts of the Bhonsla were vain, and I did not deem it convenient to conclude a peace that was not to our advantage.

Shortly ago, this enemy sent me a proposal through Sambhaji Raja that I should restore to him Rarim and Neutim and should choose one of the provinces that I had in my possession, leaving [37] him all the rest; the Bhonsla indeed offered me Alorna; as amongst them no title is assumed in connection with any territories without receiving their revenue, he thought that because His Most Faithful Majesty was pleased to confer on me the title, it followed that I should get the revenue of that district, and I would, therefore, more readily agree to a peace that would contribute to my profit. I permitted him to labour under this mistake, and replied that I was ready to treat of peace on the terms that I had offered him at Rarim, to which he had agreed, [38] and it was his secretary who interrupted it by suddenly raising his camp while he was engaged in a negotiation so important; as about this time Your Excellency arrived at this port, I got no more response. I suppose that after some time, and after having sent some astute persons to observe and explore the intention of Your Excellency, in which practice the Asiatics are notorious, he will propose to Your Excellency a settlement, as vague to start with as hitherto it has been, till the intentions of Your Excellency are ascertained, which by all means should be concealed from him.

Before passing on I must tell Your Excellency the reasons that obliged me not to prosecute the conquest of the entire dominion of the Dessais of Kudal, so that you may regulate this affair as you think best, and afterwards I shall declare what I judge more suitable in this affair. All the conquest that we (may) attempt in the country of this or any other enemy, that may not be on the seashore, is likely to be more injurious than useful to us; and if I attempted and obtained the stronghold of Alorna in the interior of the enemy country, it was because two conditions favoured my plan. First, because we could reach the place with ships by a big river and carry provisions, ammunition and other military stores without loading them on the backs of the *begarins*,* secondly because it is situated in the

* " A person pressed to carry a load, or do other work

interior of the country, and as it is one of the strongest fortresses which was formerly attacked in vain on two occasions, I thought if God blessed our arms we would strike a hammer on the Bhonsla's head and reduce his pride and the contempt with which he treated us, and it would facilitate other enterprises of mine [39]. It also seemed to me that if I removed myself far from the seacoast or from strongholds situated near navigable rivers, whence we could be easily reinforced (succoured). I should place the reputation of (our) arms in great hazard, and (expose) ourselves to the risk of being cut off, the country being mountainous, full of forests and defiles, and the roads (are) such that goats alone can with difficulty penetrate into them, and it was almost impossible to render our plans practicable with the few men we have, who hardly suffice for getting the strongholds garrisoned, and will never enable us to put into the field a considerable force. I also thought, that the enemy had dismantled the fortifications of Kudal, and Varym* was an open place, which we could not fortify without great expense and ample time, and it was better to leave this enemy that portion of the coun-

really or professedly for public service. In some provinces *begār* is the forced labour, and *bigāri* the pressed man; whilst in Karnāta, *begāri* is the performance of the lowest village offices without money payment, but with remuneration in grain or land." (Yule and Burnell. *Hobson Jobson*, pp. 80-81.)

* Vadi is the chief town of the Savantvadi state and Kudal is thirteen miles north of Vadi.

try he occupied than to expose (ourselves) to an enemy more powerful; either Angria or the Maratha might, on a pretence of help, occupy it, and we might thus have a neighbour who would cause us greater anxiety in future. On these grounds, I am of opinion, that we should never penetrate farther into the enemy land; because, if in Europe [40] a similar expedition is always perilous, even when all imaginable cunning precautions are taken, it is much more so in Asia, as the country favours sallies and surprises, and a corps, so small as ours, has no troops to expose except in the last extremity.

If the Bhonsla comes to terms, and is so reduced as to cede all the district from Sanquelim* to the river of Arandem, with the fort of Tiracol,† situated on the opposite bank of this river, in which are included the strongholds of Bicholim‡ and Alorna, with the province of Pernem,§ we can give him in return the strongholds of Rarim and Neutim, which have no port, and are situated in an open coast, where the ships are exposed and unsafe.

[41] In the districts, that this enemy may cede us, it is very necessary that those of the Ranes‖

* The district of Sanquelim lies to the north of Goa and is about 4½ leagues from the capital.

† See Note, p. 214, *infra*.

‡ & § Bicholim and Pernem are districts in the Novas Conquistas, or New Conquests. Both the districts form part of the Judicial Circle of Bardes.

‖ The Ranes and other Desais of the conquered districts took their oath of allegiance to the crown of Portu-

should also be included, principally that of Satroji Rane, Zalba Rane and Vitoba Rane and others of this family, for they form a key to the Ghats, by which way the Balaghat men usually come with their goods to the custom house of Sanquelim, and with the peace it can give us a good revenue that exceeds nine thousand Xerafins at present.

[42] Should Your Excellency, by any chance, be in any way obliged to make peace without all the advantages mentioned above, and the enemy persist in not relinquishing to this State more than one of the conquered provinces, as he has lately proposed to me, I cannot come to any decision about its choice, because, the province of Pernem, which extends from Alorna to the river of Arandem, is most important in respect of that river, where we can assemble the Pals and Gallivats in all seasons with the greatest safety; and even if by the conclusion of this treaty we cannot keep the fort of Tiracol, we could build another on the bank opposite the southern side, that might serve as a bridle to the same river and prevent the raids of this pirate, as such neighbourhood should prejudice more than any other the trade of Goa. On the other hand the

gal and the Viceroy in return guaranteed their rights and privileges in October, 1746. Papers relating to this have been published by Judice Biker. (*Tratados da India*, Vol. VI, pp. 263-272.) The Ranes belong to a warlike race and they caused their Portuguese suzerains no inconsiderable trouble in the past. The insurrection of Dipu Rane is still remembered by old men of Sanquelim.

provinces of Sanquelim and Bicholim I count equally important, no less for being very near to our district than for containing such profitable villages as Mahem, Bicholim, Mulgão, Calapur, etc.; and it is this region by which come [43] the commodities of the land of Balaghat that form the revenue of the villages of Sanquelim and Bicholim, as I have said above.

I have reason to apprehend that while I am here the Bhonslas will not make any proposal; for they fear that Your Excellency may have the goodness to listen to my opinion, and perhaps may like to follow it, which they assume will be contrary to their interests; and also because, before concluding a treaty with Your Excellency, they will attempt, as usual, to observe and examine the inclination of Your Excellency, with a view to ascertain the means and devices that they must use to induce Your Excellency to agree to a peace. To secure an advantageous peace, I think it is best, that neither our friends nor our enemies should be able to find out the decision Your Excellency arrives at. It will suit you best to pretend at first that you are (engaged) in an altogether different affair or that you are totally indifferent; it is of the utmost importance that Your Excellency should not be the party to propose the terms to the enemy, but you should compel him to present them clearly and distinctly, as otherwise the negotiation will be prolonged eternally, because he will not fail to demand such explanations of every word of Your Excellency and to seek such subterfuge in every phrase as will render it an indefinitely long process to come to an agreement about any of these (terms).

[44] To avoid such delay, the best way is that the enemy should make a proposal, article by article, and Your Excellency should respond categorically, and laconically in the margin against each of these (whether it is) "conceded" or "not conceded." In similar cases I used sometimes not to concede one of the less important clauses, so that the enemy might insist on it with great force, and after a long time I granted him the favour of abandoning my resolution, in order to avoid conceding more difficult clauses: at other times it was found convenient, according to the nature of the business, to leave it to the salutary influence of time, and in the interval the pettifoggery and the falsehood of the Hindus used to be revealed better. Experience will show Your Excellency, that all business proposed by them, be they friends or enemies, are either unjust according to all lights, or are founded only on their own interest; as they are not illuminated by the light of faith, they do not keep it either with friends or with their near relations; and as they give little or no exercise to the moral virtues, none of them are frank or sincere. Your Excellency should totally distrust the person, who for proposing to you any business, begins by adulation, flattery, profound submission and protestation of sincerity and cordial affection, and you may hold that he is firmly resolved not to fulfil anything he promises.

I have already told Your Excellency of one of the ministers of the court of Satara, called Nana, son and heir of Baji Rao, who conquered the Province of the North, and is a Brahman by caste. He is the most powerful among the Marathas in troops and money. With this chief we maintain a nominal peace, concluded at [45] Punem (Poona), capital of the same prince, four days' way from Satara, in the time of Sehhor Vis Rei Conde de Sam Domil.* I

* Dom Pedro Mascarenhas, Conde de Sandomil, governed Portuguese India as Viceroy from 1732 to 1741. It was during his regime that the Marathas annexed the Province of the North, invaded the province of Goa and threatened the very existence of the Portuguese power in India. The treaty, referred to above, was concluded in 1740. The Portuguese text is to be found in Biker, *Tratados da India*, Vol. VI, pp. 202-205. The following summary of the principal clauses are quoted from Danvers (*Portuguese in India*, Vol. II, pp. 415-16). "The Balaji Baji Rao Pradane agreed to withdraw his troops from Salsette and Bardes, and to deliver the fort of Coculim to the Portuguese in the same condition in which it was captured; the city of Daman and the fort of S. Hieronimo were to be retained by the Portuguese, who were to receive also from Baji Rao the Pergunnah Naer; the Portuguese agreed not to interfere with the jurisdiction of Bassein, Daman, Salsette, Bellaflor, Karanja, Chaul, and Morro, * * * nor to concern themselves with the districts of Ponda, Zambaulim, Panchamal, Saundem and Bidnur; they further agreed to assist Baji Rao with their fleets, should the latter be at war with the Angria; and to deliver up the city of Chaul, with all its artillery and ammunition. The gates of Chaul

call it a nominal ptace, because, he always takes the opportunity of attacking our frigates of the north, and makes this attack without respecting that treaty, and excuses himself with specious pretexts when satisfaction is demanded of him. Sometimes (the pretext is) that the flag was not noticed, on other (occasions) it was the negligence of the captains of his fleet, and other excuses, equally frivolous and false.

This winter he contemplated to surprise from us Daman, as Your Excellency is aware from letters of the Governor of that stronghold; such is the sworn guarantee of that peace, and it forms the most authentic proof of the treacherous spirit in the dealings of the Hindus. Your Excellency must look upon Nana as the greatest and the most terrible enemy of this State. The Hindus are as false and dissimulating as they are cautious and suspicious, because they judge by their scant faith the faith of others. Nevertheless the natural remorse or sense (though obscured) of Nana, does not leave him without being convinced that he is an unjust (faithless) possessor of our Province of the

were to be guarded by the British troops until advices should be received that the people of Baji Rao had retired from Salsette and Bardes." The Marathas were expected not to molest the Portuguese subjects of Salsette and Bardes. Danver's summary is misleading in respect of this part of clause 3 of the treaty. Dom Francisco, Baron Galenfels, proceeded to Puna to negotiate this treaty on behalf of the Goa Government.

North; and this anxiety causes him an uneasiness on account of the fear that sooner or later we can recover it, and to avoid being surprised in this enterprise, he sends Gallivats to Melondim in the beginning of the spring and sends into [46] this country a large number of spies to inform him immediately by sea and land of our movements. As he plays the step-father to the stronghold of Daman, it is not only on the abovementioned occasion that he attempted to take possession of it, (but) on various other occasions also he placed his fleet outside the bar of that port to embarrass its trade and the supply of provision, and he prohibited its introduction by land to reduce the place by famine; and whenever his fear increases he marches up to the crest of the Ghats, threatening to come down either for embarrassing the reinforcement of the stronghold or for the conquest of the province. For the same reason he has kept the Bhonsla in the hope that he will help him against us, but he never puts his promise into effect. He fears so much that this enemy (the Bhonsla) may conclude a peace with us, that there is no art or scheme he will not use to prevent it, because so long as we are engaged with him (the Bhonsla) Nana's suspicion is lulled to rest. The Bhonsla wants the help of Nana in a different form. The latter had already resolved to give him help with the intention of taking possession of the whole of his country, so that he might be nearer us and harass us with greater facility. The Bhonsla penetrated into this intention, and being afraid of such help in troops, suggested that it should be commuted into money, so that he might purchase other (troops) more reliable than his. I fomented, as much as I could, this suspicion, and when he threatened me with Nana's assistance, I retorted, that it would be favourable to me, because seizing, as Nana intended, all the Bhonsla country, he would only avenge this State on the greatest enemy that it ever had.

One of the most popular generals, to whom Nana has hitherto entrusted his army, is Ramchandra Malhar,* who absented himself from the

* "Ramchundur Baba Shenwee, a person to whom, although his conduct was extremely exceptionable, especially in the manner by which he obtained power, the Mahratta country is much indebted. This person, originally known by the name of Ramchundur Mulhar, was Koolkurnee of the village of Aroolee, subject to the Sawunts of Waree, from whose power he was obliged to flee as a defaulter in the revenues of his village. He came to Satara, when he was taken into the service of Kucheswur Baba Uleekur, and by him recommended to Bajee Rao, under whom he distinguished himself, both as a soldier and a man of business. Bajee Rao appointed him Dewan to Ranoojee Sindia, and it partly accounts for Ranoojee's proverbial poverty that Ramchundur made a large fortune. At Ranoojee's death he bribed Sewdasheo Rao Bhow, in hopes of being continued by his interest as the Dewan of Jayapa; but as Jayapa disliked him, and Mulhar Rao Holkar opposed the arrangement, the Peishwa removed him from the situation." (Grant-Duff, *History of the Mahrattas*, Oxford edition, Vol. I, pp. 448-49.) Sadashiva Rao Bhau then appointed Ramchandra his own Dewan, which office he retained till his death. His son

country of the Bhonsla, whose vassal he was, on account of some trouble and injury, and accepted that service in which he made himself as esteemed as opulent. His heart is so noble, that forgetting, for the benefit of his own country, the injustice with which he had been treated there, he has secretly helped the Bhonsla with considerable sums of money. Now I am assured that the said Ramchandra has some misunderstanding with Nana.

Shortly after making myself familiar with this country I recognised the great and inevitable advantage that the enemies have over us; as it is easy for them to be informed of any of our movements, [47] (while) we cannot in convenient time get news of theirs. There lives in our country a large number of Moors and Hindus, of the same colour, the same habits, the same language and the same law as those of the enemy land, where are also settled many (people), Christians more in name than in reality; they are all more loyal to the enemies than to us. They enter and leave this country, no disguise being necessary for them, to verify whatever they like; the Portuguese, however, cannot succeed in it, because neither the turban nor the tunic (cabaya) can conceal them, and their language and colour betray them most readily. Dom Antonio José Henriques took refuge in the court of Satara for a crime of which he was accused at Goa,

Sadashiv Ramchandra enjoyed the confidence of his father's patron and played an important part in Maratha politics.

and by his genial and jovial disposition and knowledge of the language earned the favour of Shahu, and contracted an intimate friendship with some of his ministers. I decided to use him for getting information of that court, where are formed the projects to be executed by the armies destined for different quarters. This enabled me on many occasions to be on my guard and take precautionary measures. Through him [48] I caused certain maxims to be spread in that court which contributed to our tranquillity and to introduce into the heart of Shahu a doubt about permitting a vassal like Nana to augment his forces and fortune, who could cause him anxiety both in life and death, as he had no hope of succession. Nana was persuaded that to help the Bhonsla was contrary to his interests, because the more firmly I established myself in his territories the better should I be weaned from the memory of the loss of the Province of the North. With these and similar other suggestions, that time and occasions offered, I managed to enquire into the dispositions and the mind of the Marathas. One of the Ministers of Satara, called Ganaxama,* whose office corresponds to that of the Secretary of State, professes friendship for this State, having inherited

* Naro Ram was a Shenvi or Saraswat Brahman. He was originally Kulkarni of Kochre near Sawantvadi. About 1707 he entered the service of Dhanaji Jadhava and in 1713 he was appointed Mantri by Shahu. He died in 1748 and was succeeded in his office by Ghanashyam Narayan, his nephew and adopted son.

from his uncle Naro Ram his office and goodwill. Ganaxama's daughter has been married to a son of Vithoji Sinay Dumo,* our subject and an inhabitant of the island of Combarjua, by which way people sometimes go up to Satara. This Hindu is one of the smartest and acutest, and, Your Excellency should, therefore, take every care to secure from him information in such a manner that he may never find out how Your Excellency receives it. Ganaxama always kept with me, and I with him, a friendly correspondence; he solicited me to use my influence with the King of Sunda so that he might give him a village in the province of Phonda, in the neighbourhood of Salsette, contiguous [49] to the Pagoda of Queula,† of which he is a devotee. Without excusing myself from the good offices with the King, I went on prolonging this negotiation with specious pretexts, in order not to displease him, but with a firm purpose of persuading the King of Sunda to the contrary, because it suits neither him nor this State that a powerful Maratha should have a footing and

* Vithoji Sinai Dumo was on many occasions employed as envoy to neighbouring Hindu princes. He was for some time farmer of the rent of Bicholim and Sanquelim, and also served as Mazumdar of the custom house of Sanquelim.

† Quela, in the district of Ponda, is one of the most popular places of pilgrimage for the Hindus of Goa. It is said that the image of Shantadurga was transported in days of yore by thirteen Saraswat emigrants from their original home near Bengal. The temple has been munificently endowed by the Kings of Sunda.

make his residence at a place that in future may cause anxiety to both of these dominions.

I have given an account of the potentates with whom this State has relations, either as friends or as enemies; it remains now to explain to Your Excellency the manner in which the Asiatics wage war and the means I used to defend myself against them.

Your Excellency should not think that the troops of the Marathas and other princes, about whom rumour has spread with the progress of time in this part as well as in Asia and Europe, are more formidable than a similar number of disorderly people of that sort. From what experience I already have of them, I would have no hesitation with a corps of five thousand regular troops to attack such an army of fifty thousand. The disorder, that exists in their array, they observe even in marching and encampment. Their camp differs little from that of the Gypsies; each one finds out a place, a shade or a tree that suits him best, they have little vigilance of guards and sentinels, and are, in this respect, liable to be surprised very easily. This militia is divided into three corps, Cavalry, Infantry and Armed elephants. The Cavalry is composed of a few good horses and a large number of sorry jades called nags. Some soldiers of this corps are armed [50] with lances, others with large swords. The Sipaes who form their infantry are armed with *Caitocas*,* which is a kind of small firearm, carried

* Large rifled muskets with ramrods of iron used by the Marathas of the Novas Conquistas. They have rings

by them more frequently than our arms. Some of them are armed with one or two broad and large swords and others with bow and arrow. An infinite number of men called Fakirs always follow the army. They are not men of arms, nor have they to fight, but they only rob and ravage the country they pass through. The elephants, taught and trained for war, are of the greatest value to the Hindus, when they are intrepid and are not frightened by noise. Princes, generals and distinguished persons mount them; they are used for charging the enemy, carrying different platoons of men armed with bow and arrow. When infuriated, they cause great harm with the trunk. There are elephants (when they have all the necessary qualities) that sell for twenty thousand [51] rupees. These troops are not such as firmly await a well disciplined enemy and attack him with an intrepid resolution. All their operations consist of sallies, surprises and abmuscades; and in woods and defiles, supposed to be safe, they are terrible, and they are much more formidable after a rout; in fine, these troops are a kind of *Pondouros** with less ferocity and courage but supremely clever in availing themselves of any disorder or advantage. Their major enterprises terminate more in causing harm, robbery and devastation of

round the barrel, to indicate the number of men killed and wounded, as a testimonial to the prowess of the owner. (Dalgado, *Glossário Luso-Asiático*, Vol. I, p. 174.)

* Pendharis.

the country than in fighting battles decided by sword and fire, for which they have great horror.

The dread that all have for the Marathas precedes their armies and announces to the provinces for which they set out, and farther still, the loss with which they are menaced. This compels them to send immediately emissaries to the armies to avoid by means of many lakhs of rupees the ruin with which they are threatened. (When) the expedition (is) finished, the armies re-assemble, without unsheathing the sword, with an immense spoil and wealth which sometimes are not equivalent to the expenses incurred for the confederate troops, to whom one rupee is paid per day per man, and five hundred rupees for each horse wounded, lost or killed in the incursion. If such troops had discipline and courage in proportion to other circumstances, they would be invincible. None endure so many hardships as these : they do not require uniforms, for they go naked from waist upward, with three or four *apas*, a kind of cake made of rice or wheat, which they get for eating for a number of days; and by [52] reason of this disparity it is spared the great embarrassment of carriages that a big army requires for carrying provisions. By extensive and repeated incursions, the Marathas have inspired such terror and panic in the whole of Asia from the Indus to the Ganges, that absolutely all yield to them and none resist them. On several occasions they arrived to touch with the points of their lances the ramparts of Delhi and Agra, capitals of the Great Moghul. The kingdom of Cambay and Gujrat, the provinces of Arcot and the Carnatic, and the whole of the district of Bengal have been recently the pitiful theatre of their destructions whence they have extorted and actually carried away immense wealth, thereby making the treasury of the said Moghul diminish considerably. As they do not wage war for glory or in defence of a just cause, but for mere ambition and gain of money, they are not easily inclined, unless they have some particular end (in view), to descend from the Ghats into the district called Concan in which is included that of Goa, for it is poor, and they cannot seize things that may satisfy their cupidity; and little do they like that the passes should be disputed [53] with steel and fire from which no profit can result but only loss of life. If they sometimes entered into the province of Salsette, the incursion was for this reason a transitory one; and the only occasion, when they stayed (there) in the year 1739, was for causing diversion, as they had undertaken the conquest of the Province of the North. In my time they never put their feet in this (district), because whenever I suspected that their army was destined for this part, I immediately ordered the defiles of the Ghats to be occupied by our sepoys and those of the King of Sunda; and sometimes I caused it to be reported that I had ordered mines and firecakes to be put in the narrow passes for which some preparations, more apparent than real, were made; and God permitted that their descent should be thus baffled.

The Bhonsla, who is also of the Maratha caste, has no different method of making war; and his sepoys are of the same quality as, or differ slightly from ours, the majority are the very cultivators of the land whom he makes to join in arms when he intends any action or surprise attack which in my time, with God's favour, was always frustrated; and I know that nothing will happen; his troops and forces need not cause us any anxiety; they cannot attempt the siege of our strongholds, because he lacks artillery and other necessary military stores. This enemy is nevertheless clever enough to exploit any disorder and to watch for any carelessness, and he is not less cunning in introducing spies and bribing people in the strongholds, which is avoided with great vigilance and caution and by transferring garrisons at uncertain times, as I have always done.

From what I have said above, it will be seen that this enemy is to be neither dreaded nor despised : news will continually reach Your Excellency from all parts, of the mobilisation of his troops, of the re-inforcement he has received and of similar other (things), to which Your Excellency should not give credit; nor should Your Excellency refrain from taking precautions as if they were correct, but so quietly, that the public may not perceive that they cause you any anxiety. From what (information) Your Excellency has already received in this short interval, and seeing how shallow they prove, Your

Excellency will be able to judge for the future, what opinion to form.

Before concluding with the friendly and hostile Hindus of whom I have hitherto treated, I must inform Your Excellency of some points that to me appear essential.

[54]. When the Sr. Marquis de Louriçal took this Government for the second time, he found Ponda, and Goddo, which serve as its citadel, occupied by the Marathas, as also the stronghold of Sanguem situated upon the river that flows by Rachol and adjoins to the Ghats of Tinem and Diguim;* he very wisely resolved to expel the enemy from our neighbourhood, and started with Sanguem which he attacked and demolished, (and then) turned with his troops against Ponda, which met the same fate. Goddo however remained in the enemy's possession; entrusted with its command, Ismal Can,† a Mahomedan general, sought

* Both these ghats lie in the districts formerly belonging to the Raja of Sunda. The village of Tinai is thirty miles north-west of Supa in the North Kanara District of Bombay.

† Ismal Khan is invariably styled as valoroso or valiant by the Portuguese and he is frequently mentioned in contemporary political and historical pamphlets on Indian subjects. He was evidently a soldier of fortune and received his early training in Angria's service. Ismal Khan entered Portuguese service during the Viceroyalty of the Marquis of Alorna and was ultimately promoted to the command of ten galleys. He inflicted two defeats on the Chief of

to sell it to anyone who might offer him the best terms. He negotiated with the Bhonsla about its delivery, to frustrate which we requested the King of Sunda to propose terms to Ismal Can; the pacts were solemnised on both sides with the same assurance, and in this manner Goddo returned to its former sovereign. On our part we restored to Sunda the demolished strongholds. These events took place when the Sr. Marquis, already prostrated by the illness of which he died, had no time to plan other conquests than those of the eternity. The Government that succeeded his, either for lack of experience or for other causes, did not attend to the future, nor did they secure the advantage that circumstances and opportunity at that time offered for clearing and extending [55] our dominion. They were contented with forty thousand Xerafins that the King of Sunda gave for the expenses of this expedition, presuming to have rendered an important service.

In my opinion the errors committed on that occasion were many: the first was to demolish Sanguem, while its preservation was very important for us, for it is by that site that the enemy usually make their entrance into the province of Salsette

Sawantvadi and one on the Arab fleet as we learn from an undated pamphlet by Feliz Feliciano da Fonseca entitled *Relacao de hum grande combate e victoria, que contra o Gentio e Arabio consequio a Armada que do porto de Goa sahio de Guarda costa, em Julho de 1753 commandada pelo valoroso Ismal Can, commandante de dez gallias.*

and it is a short way from the Ghats whence they descend. Occupied by us, it would serve as an arsenal for keeping arms with men and provision; and in case of the enemy passing by it, it would be very important to maintain in the rear of their army a stronghold that would embarrass their convoys, and we would remain in possession of the whole of the river of Rachol. The second was that if we could negotiate with Ismal Khan about the surrender of Goddo, we might garrison it with our men and this would render Sunda more submissive to us and leave us free from the anxiety that the Marathas should come back to occupy the place, it being so near to Goa and in the hands of Sunda. I think it would be possible for us by this means to take possession of the whole of the province of Ponda, which would be expedient for us, as it is very rich, and from this province we may continually receive the benefit of much necessary provisions; and because if necessity compels us, on account of its vicinity, to defend it at our cost against any invasion, it will be much more convenient to possess it as our own and add its revenue to that of our Government, than to leave it to one who needs our help to preserve and defend the province; but should we agree to leave it to Sunda, it ought in any case to be in exchange of and for the restitution of Cabo da Rama, of which the King of Sunda [56] long ago unjustly took possession, it being a part of the province of Salsette. And even to-day there are persons who recollect it to have been always united with that province, and we may recover the *foros*, we may also be able to oblige Sunda to cede the fort of Piro and the Bay of Gales and the river of Ancola,* that cause so much trouble to our smaller vessels by their claims which are continually charged in those ports; and it may serve also as a curb on the Sunda that he may not attempt piracy, which he practises (almost) safely against us, inspite of a friendly peace. This occasion, so opportune and favourable, was spoiled, so that Goddo may now keep us in continuous anxiety, should the current news prove true, that Nana intends to deprive Sambhaji Raja of Kolhapur and the whole of his kingdom, and take possession of the said Goddo (with a view) to oppress us and to molest us from closer quarters. In that case Your Excellency will find yourself obliged to make at the same time all exertions for defending it (Goddo) as well for getting possession of Melondim, as I have said before, so that Nana may not be so near us by land and sea. We shall now pass to the mode of defence.

Your Excellency, finds yourself in a country where are found all imaginable advantages for its defence: Ours is divided into three parts; the first is the island of Goa, and the adjacent islands and the

* **Both the creek of Gales and the river of Ankola are in the North Kanara District of Bombay. Ankola is about fifteen miles south-east of Karwar. The river is also called the Sankhadole.**

other [57]two are the provinces of Bardez and Salsette: the first is washed on one side by the ocean, from Chapora to Agoada* and on the other by a mighty river that disembogues itself in the sea and separates it from the island of Goa.† On the side facing the enemy land it is defended by a strong wall little more than a quarter of [58] a league from the new fort (Forto Novo) to Coluale, a work of Sr. Conde de Linhares.‡ In this line are included the abovementioned fort (with) those [59] of Tivim, Meio and Coluale, with a ditch, which was commenced but not completed. It could easily turn this province [60] into an island. In the same province is situated on a high mountain of natural strength the fortress of Agoada that defends the entrance to the Bar of [61] Goa; if the ditch, that was begun in Sinquerim had been extended, it could also be easily turned into an island. In this province is also situated the fort of Reis§ which transverses (the river) with the artillery of the fort of Gaspar Dias,‖ [62] situated in the island of Goa, for obstructing the passage

* Agoada is opposite Pangim on the other bank of the Mandovy.

† The river Mandovy, which flows by Pangim, so called because the custom house stood on its banks.

‡ Dom Miguel de Noronha, Conde de Linhares, served as Viceroy from 1629 to 1635.

§ Reis Magos, on the right bank of the Mandovy, opposite Gaspar Dias.

‖ The fort of Gaspar Dias was about a mile from Pangim or Nava Goa. The fort has been demolished.

through the shoal (that is found) at the entrance of that bar. The province of Salsette is most exposed to the invasions of the enemy on the side of the Ghats, and if our sepoys and natives were resolute, the descent by the rugged defiles of the lands of Sunda would be difficult. The stronghold of Rachol, though irregular, is, none the less, sufficiently strong for all Asiatic enemies; during my regime I ordered a wet ditch to be made and it has the facility of inundating the entire country round about on the side of Curtorim and of the island of the Jesuits without leaving for (enemy) attack more than a small space on an eminence on that side where the fortress is stronger. In this province is also situated the fortress of [63] Mormugão,* that defends the bar of that river which separates Goa from the said province, a work of Your Excellency's grandfather, the Senhor Conde de Alvor.†

The island of Goa, the largest of all, is washed on two sides by two mighty (caudeloso) rivers, which, divided into several channels, form the adjacent islands, with which I shall deal below; the only dry ford, that these rivers have, is in front of S. Braz, and is defended by the fort of that name; at the farthest end where stands the fort of Cabo, which defends the bar, it is enclosed by the ocean; then

* Marmugão has a fine harbour. It is about an hour's journey from Pangim by sea. Marmugão forms the terminus of the railway that connects the province of Goa with British India.

† Francisco de Tavora, Conde de Alvor, was Viceroy from 1681 to 1686.

follow the fort of Gaspar Dias, of which mention has already been made above, and the bridge of Pangim* [64] a work of Sr. V. Rei Conde De Linhares that serves as a barricade and impediment to the enemies. The walls, first begun by Sr. V. Rei D' Antao de Noronha† and continued by other Viceroys, run [65] from the fort of Daugim by S. Braz and S. Thiago,‡ whence [66] they turn by Mangueiral,§ S. João Sagu‖ and continue as far as the gates of Moula, terminating within a short distance of the magazine (casa de polvora) above the hill that dominates it; two thousand men cannot garrison its vast extent; it is an imperfect structure, ruined at several places in course of time: on the side facing Salsette the whole shore is defended by some fascines where it is easier to disembark and at a place called D. Paula;¶ care should be taken to avoid any surprise by the side of the sea.

* The bridge of Pangim, otherwise known as bridge Linhares still exists and connects Ribandar with Pangim. The greater portion of the structure looks more like a causeway than like a bridge.

† Dom Antao de Noronha served as Viceroy from 1564 to 1568.

‡ The fortress of S. Thiago has long been abandoned.

§ Mangueiral is now in ruins.

‖ Saint John Sahagu is the guardian saint of the church of Corlim. The Church was built by Archbishop Aleixo de Menezes between 1596 and 1610.

¶ A plantation that derived its name from the owner, Dona Paula. It forms part of the village of Taleigão, on the Marmugão river.

Above the church of Pangim, is a spacious ground possessing the greatest advantages that can be desired, so that in case the enemies enter Goa they cannot continue there. It has a [67] natural esplanade on all sides, equally dominating all the circumjacent country, without any eminence that can be used for attack; in it terminates the bridge of Pangim, through which it will be impossible for the enemy to pass if a small redoubt is made in front of it at Ribandar* and another at the end, for, one side of this bridge is defended by a mighty river and the other by an inundated ground broken by saltpits;† it is near the bar from where its provisioning can be looked (after); in that beach bigger and smaller vessels can remain secure and sheltered against all storms; and it is the best situation where the customhouse ought to have been to avoid the evasions (deviation) that can be practised among the canals. After I reconnoitred this ground I noticed that it would be the only and real refuge of the forces of Goa, should the enemy invade it, and they would not be able to persist in the city so long as we maintained ourselves in that site. Would to God that the engineers, who inspired Sr. Conde de Alvor to make the immense expense [68] that was incurred at Mormugão, had applied the money to this place, it would suffice to ruin the

* Ribandar is very near Pangim and is connected with that city by the bridge already mentioned.

† The description holds good even now.

hopes of any enemy of ever taking possession of this capital.

The adjacent islands are: the island of Divar, popularly called Piedade, where the enemy will never enter (even) in the most calamitous times, because the channels surrounding it offer no ford and on the side facing the main land it is defended by the fort of Narua* which plays with its artillery upon the whole of the river on that side; the isle of Chorão, has the river only on the side towards the main land; it is ill defended by a fort which stands at a great distance.

The two islands of Palem (*alias* Ponelem) and Corjuem, are very near the main land, and where the channel is very narrow, they are defended by the fort of the latter island. The island of Santo Estevam has two fords, one of them is defended by a fort whence the shots have little effect, [69] the open batteries, situated near by, serve as a greater defence to both the fords. The island of Combarjua, is most exposed to invasions, because the canal, that separates it from Goa as well as from the country of Sunda, is very narrow and at low tide can be easily forded; the side facing Goa is well defended by the fort of S. Braz, and on the side towards Sunda, I ordered to make a barricade of compact gabions and a battery for its defence.

* The fort is now in ruins. It was situated in the third parish of the isle of Divar.

**

The fords and dry passages can be easily defended with open batteries over them and with Manchuas posted on either side of those fords to sweep them over with artillery, and for preventing the injury from the fleet to those who guard the coast, in case the Baloons for fear of the enemy come by the rivers at night, this precaution will suffice; for the enemy, who greatly dread our fire would not attempt it, if the passage of the fords is rendered difficult at low tide, for fear that the tide may return if any delay is made, and they would be lost and cut off if they remained.

These advantages, that in other lands would be desired for defending posts with few men and moderate resolution, are rendered useless in this country by the pusillanimity of the inhabitants, for, even if they were so safe as in the castle of Milan, to hear a trumpet* (rabana) of the enemy or a rumour of their appearance, even at a great distance, would alone suffice for them to fly a hundred leagues thence, without any human power being able to restrain them, much less if they perceived the least foundation for their dread. Sometimes this inconvenience is avoided by posting regular troops in the most dangerous places and the natives in places of less risk, or in [70] ships, whence they cannot have the liberty to fly, with some military officers and a few soldiers, who check them.

* *Rabana* also means an orchestra, consisting of ordinary drums, kettle drums, clarions and a big trumpet called *singa*.

INDEX

B

D

F

G

H

L

M

N

T

U

V

W

ERRATA

p. 12 lines 24-25 *for* Polbora *read* Polvora.

p. 24 line 1 *for* 1768 *read* 1678.

p. 28 line 25 *for* 1789 *read* 1679.

p. 30 line 3 *for* Shankheswar *read* Sangameswar.

p. 42 line 11 *for* 1681 *read* 1686.

p. 52 line 16 *for* Bisholy *read* Bicholy.

p. 64 line 10 *for* year *read* century.

p. 92 line 20 *for* Shekoji *read* Sekhoji.

p. 130 line 4 *for* Narranji *read* Narun Gi.

p. 158 line 10 *for* Nâimâ *read* Nâimâr.

OPINIONS

" Times of India " on Dr. Sen's Works.

With one statement made by Lord Meston it would be impossible to quarrel. He referred to the new school of Indian investigators, "versed in modern criticism and exploring the field with honesty and sincerity," which he regards as one of the best fruits of the new Nationalist movement. With historians like D. R. Bhandarkar, **Surendranath Sen,** * * * —to mention only a few of those who have done admirable work—India may well claim to have established a school of research worthy of herself and her past history. *Times of India*, quoted in the *Pioneer* of Friday, May 20, 1921, mofussil edition.

ADMINISTRATIVE SYSTEM OF THE MARATHAS

Prof. A. Beriedale Keith: I have now had the opportunity of reading your treatise on the Administrative System of the Marathas. It contains a very large amount of interesting information, carefully put together, and rendered illuminating by comparison with the description of early Hindu institutions derived from the Dharmasastra literature. It undoubtedly sheds much light on the course of administration prior to the advent of British supremacy, and the impartiality and good sense of such personal judgments as you express deserve recognition.

Prof. Jules Bloch (*Journal Asiatique*): C'est un ouvrage solide et important, qui fait houneur á l'auteur et á l'ecole á laquelle il se rattache.

C. H. Keith Jopp: I think it will prove useful to the student of Maratha history.

The Hon'ble Justice C. A. Kincaid: I have spent several delightful hours reading your most valuable work 'Administrative System of the Marathas.' It is full of erudition and should long remain the classic text on the subject. I do not fancy any one else would have the industry as well as the learning, to write another such book. I congratulate you warmly on your great achievement."

S. M. Edwards (*The Indian Antiquary, January, 1924*): Much original research in Maratha history has been conducted of late years by Indian scholars, who have thrown a flood of light upon the circumstances and character of the administration founded by Shivaji and subsequently usurped by the Peshwas. In this respect the work of men like the late Professor H. G. Limaye and Messrs. Rajwade, Sardesai, Parasnis and others has been invaluable. Dr. Surendranath Sen has already established his authority in the same field by his excellent translation of the bakhar of Krisnaji Anant Sabhasad, which is unquestionably the most credible and trusworthy of the various old chronicles of Shivaji's life and reign. He has now placed students of Maratha affairs under a further obligation by this careful exposition of the administrative system in vogue in the Deccan in the pre-British period.

The value of his latest work seems to us to lie in its impartiality and in its careful avoidance of extreme diction in cases where the author's views differ from those already expressed by both English and Indian writers. He treats Grant Duff and Ranade with equal impartiality, and does not hesitate to point out their errors of deduction: he appreciates fully the good features of Shivaji's institutions but is equally explicit as to their short-comings: and he devotes a distinct section of his work to explaining by carefully chosen quotations and examples that much of Shivaji's administrative machinery was not a new product of his unquestionably resourceful mind, but had its roots deep down in ancient Hindu lore.

As to the actual facts disclosed in Dr. Sen's work, their number is so many and they are so interesting that it is hardly possible to deal with them in the brief compass of a review.

In conclusion, let it suffice to remark that Dr. Sen has produced an admirable work of reference for students of the history of the Deccan in the seventeenth and eighteenth centuries.

G. S. Sardesai (*Vividha Jnan Vistar*): All students of Maratha history must read the works of Dr. Sen.

Rao Bahadur Kashinath Narayan Sane: I hasten to congratulate you on your having so systematically and so lucidly brought together all the information available on the subject of the administration of the country under the Maratha Rulers."

Sir Verney Lovett (*The Asiatic Review*): The book contains much interesting information.

R. A. Leslie Moore (*Bulletin of the School of Oriental Studies, London Institutions*): This book is the result of wide and careful study of original documents, chiefly Marhatta and English, and only needs a more comprehensive glossary.

The Times Literary Supplement (*Thursday, May 10, 1923*): As in the case of the Great Napoleon, Shivaji the Conqueror has always been more attractive to historians than Shivaji the Administrator, and less than justice has been done to his constructive ability. Dr. Surendranath Sen has written a scholarly analysis of the Maratha administration under Shivaji and the Peshwas, and in spite of a natural bias in favour of his own countrymen he can claim to have proved that the Maratha Government will at least bear favourable comparison with, and was in some respects superior to, those of contemporary Europe.

Journal of the Royal Asiatic Society (*October, 1924*): Dr. Surendranath Sen has given us a most careful and comprehensive work and has shown that the work begun so well by Ranade is being continued in competent hands. The fact that the Maratha kingdom lasted for a century and a half should be sufficient to dispel the idea that the Marathas were mere bands of marauders. It comes as a surprise, however, to see what a wealth of material there is for the study of their constitutional and administrative history. The author investigates the origin and development of their institutions, analysing the influence of traditional Hindu systems of polity and of those of their Muslim neighbours. The book is a most valuable addition to the publications of Calcutta University."

Times of India (*15th August, 1923*): We can hardly find adequate words in which to express our approval of this work and our admiration of the writer's industry. * *

Here we must leave Dr. Sen's fascinating book. Besides its immense value, it throws a curious light on the difficulties which to-day confront an Indian writer. Dr. Sen is a Bengali. In order to obtain a hearing he has to write in English. But he who writes on Maratha history must be conversant both with Marathi and Persian. Dr. Sen promptly learnt these two difficult languages. His work is thus a monument to his wonderful linguistic gifts as well as to his tireless unceasing industry.

Pioneer (*Sunday, the 2nd September, 1923*): The most noticeable characteristic of this book is a pleasing sobriety of judgment. We have seen much of history written rather from the standpoint of present politics than of past happenings, and we heartily welcome the thoroughly impartial standpoint which Dr. Sen assumes. We are disposed to congratulate him the more warmly, in that the Maratha period of Indian history offers an almost irresistible temptation to the 'patriotic' scholar to discover what is not to be found, and to interpret hard realities in the light of glowing aspirations. The author has confined himself to two principal tasks: he desires, in the first place, to defend Maratha rule from some of the aspersions ignorantly cast upon it; and he traces the connection between the salient features of Maratha institutions and the traditional characteristics of the typical Hindu polity. We may say at once that he has discharged both these tasks with learning, moderation, and a rare sense of historical perspective. * * * We congratulate Dr. Sen upon an excellent and most scholarly piece of work.

The Englishman (*Tuesday, 5th June, 1923*): Displaying an impartial spirit, the author has embodied the results of his five years' toil into a very readable volume which is well up to the traditions of modern historians.

Bombay Chronicle (*Sunday, 10th June, 1923*): The work is bound to be interesting to students of history as well as sociology, though it is neither purely a history nor even a social study. * * On the whole the book is well worth study from what ever standpoint one approaches it.

Rangoon Mail (*Friday, 8th February, 1924*): In Dr. Surendranath Sen, M.A., Ph.D., Lecturer in Maratta History and Marathi Literature and author of Administrative system of the Marhattas (from original sources), we have one more evidence of the genuine spirit of historical research that abounds in the Bengal of to day. * * * The Volume is a thoroughly enjoyable one and has the supreme merit of avoiding extra-learned spurious technicality. We welcome the author because he is an honest student of Indian history: we welcome him because he has the art of simple narration: we welcome him because he has really studied his source in a critical and comparative spirit: and we welcome him because men like him of unassuming patriotic impulse are some justification, however slight, of the foreign-ridden University Education now in vogue in this country. Dr. Sen is one of that honest group of earnest students and researchers whom Sir Asutosh Mookerjee has brought together under great handicaps in the Post-Graduate Department of the University of Calcutta and the more young men of Dr. Sen's type take up the burden of Indian historical research out of non-Indian hands, the better for the cause of Indian culture. Dr. Sen's book ought to forge one more link between the great Bengali and Marathi communities in India.

Vividha Jnan Vistar (*June, 1923*): The road indicated by the late Justice Ranade has been rendered more wide and less thorny by Professor Sen.

MILITARY SYSTEM OF THE MARATHAS

Sir William Foster: * * *
I read the work with pleasure, and was particularly glad to see that you had vindicated the Marathas from the stigma of piracy. I have upheld your doctrine in an article on Severndroog castle contributed to the February issue of *The Blue Peter.*

Sir Richard Temple (*The Indian Antiquary, Vol. LVIII, May, 1929*): It is not possible to review this important volume of deep research in the space available in this Journal, and the present notice must confine itself to a statement that not only have Maratha sources been utilised, but much of the unpublished English, French and Portuguese records as well. The work has been thoroughly and systematically performed in such a manner as to compel the attention of the reader to Dr. Surendranath Sen's conclusions, to which the special attention of all students is herein drawn.

* * * *

Dr. Sen devotes a long chapter (pp. 28-53) to chauth and sardeshmukhi, the terrible fiscal demands, which, as he says, "have been invariably associated with the Marathas as an appropriate expression of their predatory genius." He shows, however, that chauth, nominally a tax of one quarter of the revenue, was not an invention of Sivaji, as it has usually been held to be, and his remarks on the whole subject are illuminating and of the greatest interest.

The most novel parts of Dr. Sen's book are in the chapters on the Maratha Navy, which are worthy of the closest examination, as they deal with a bypath of history difficult to traverse: and he is to be congratulated on a clear and consecutive statement of a most complicated story. He considers, with a great wealth of research into obscure documents, the whole tale of the Maratha Navy from its commencement under Sivaji to its development successively under the Angrias, the Savants and the Peshwas, and its final disappearance after a not long existence. He tells the story too, in such a way that the various leaders appear severally before us as living characters in a natural sequence of men and events. This is no mean achievement, as any who—like the present writer—has tried to unravel this very tangled skein, can appreciate.

Dr. Sen dives into the vexed question of piracy versus privateering and assertion of sovereignty of the sea, with a view to showing that the Maratha seamen were no pirates, though they of course were always held to be such by their opponents, the European sailors of their time. What he has to say here has much force and should be carefully weighed by students.

*   *   *   *

The whole book is valuable in the highest sense and a good instance ot fair-minded research.

Sir Wolseley Haig (*Bulletin of the Schools of Oriental Studies, London.*) Dr. Sen has made Maratha History his special study, and is already well-known as one of the leading authorities on this subject. This beok appears to me to be the most valuable of all his works, the mature fruit of research and study. It is a minute account of Shivaji's military system, and of its development and decline, but it is much more than this, for it describes how social and political influences affected the military ideals of the Marathas, and explains very clearly the reasons for their decay as a military and political power.

* * * *

No fewer than eighty-five pages of the book are devoted to the birth of the Maratha navy under Sivaji, its growth under the Angrias, and its maturity and decay under the Peshwas. Dr. Sen concludes this naval record with an interesting chapter on "Piracy, or the Sovereignty of the Sea." This is as complete a chronicle of the naval affairs of the Marathas as I have seen.

* * * *

The book is a most valuable contribution to the history of India in the seventeenth and eighteenth centuries.

G. S. Sardesai (*The New Era, May, 1929*):

* * * * *

Tremendous capacity for labour, accurate and minute study, a pithy and terse style, often running into happy epigrammes, and a rarely sympathetic grasp of the subject, are, in my opinion, some of the outstanding merits of Dr. Sen's treatment. The book has become very readable and edifying to the general readers as well as to a specialist, and will doubtless prove a useful guide to those who would hereafter take up similar topics for special study concerning Maratha History.

* * * *

The Marathas have fallen ; but the memories of the past are an invaluable asset for the rising nation. They are a legacy left us by the great souls of Shivaji and Mahadaji ; and it behoves us all to unite and work towards producing a full, reasoned, and comprehensive account. Such a task is being slowly accomplished, and from this point of view, Dr. Sen's present work is sure to be ranked among the many valuable contributions made to the subject by writers like Duff, Ranade, and Sarkar.

Times Literary Supplement, December 13, 1928: Dr. Surendranath Sen is one of the best of the younger Indian historians, his patriotism being under control of a cautious, critical method. In the work of such men there is at last a promise that the writing of Indian history will become something better than enthusiasm or prejudice. His record of patient research justifies confidence ; he has explored carefully what is the least investigated field of Indian records and has ransacked the Portuguese manuscripts stored in Goa and Lisbon. This knowledge of the first European people in India he has supplemented by a study of the documents available in London and Paris and of an extensive literature in English, Hindi and Marathi.

Dr. Sen observes that the Marathas were "the last indigenous empire-builders of India." Something of the outline of their story remains in the memory of the Englishman interested in Indian history ; he remembers that they rose to grasp at empire, but were repulsed disastrously at the third Battle of Panipat, only to recover miraculously and swiftly and to hold in their power both Grand Mogul and Rajput chieftains. He has a vague recollection of the Mahratta Ditch outside Calcutta, and of Lake's and Wellesley's campaigns. But despite the excellent work of some of the best of all the British historians who have written about India, whole tracts of this story have dropped almost completely out of sight. For a hundred who know of Assaye there is not one who knows of Popham's marvellous capture of Gwalior or remembers from what a peril the watchful skill of Warren Hastings rescued his colleagues of the Bombay Presidency. The Sikhs gave us fiercer battles the Gurkhas a worse campaign: but the Marathas for upwards of a century remained a sturdy foe, whom defeat left still formidable. Dr. Sen examines the strands which gave their military organizations its toughness of texture and the reasons for its decay. He shows how much of weakness came from the very thing that to outward seeming gave an appearance of impressive strength—the modernizing of the Maratha forces by De Boigne and the numerous European adventurers recruited by Mahadaji Sindhia. The Marathas as infantrymen did surprisingly well: but their metamorphosis was partial, and weapons and methods of warfare remained mixed: artillery (and that rarely of the best, for it had to be purchased from European neighbours more ready to part with the obsolete than with the new and efficient) supplemented by arrows and showers of stones. These light skirmishers did best when they kept to their wiry little ponies and tactics of sudden sally and retreat. They must have seemed to their victims in league with the goblin-hosts of Siva of whom their first great leader was popularly held to be an incarnation.

* * * *"

The Journal of the Royal Asiatic Society (*April, 1929*): * * * *
The well-known author of this little book is to be congratulated on the careful study he has made of all available materials bearing on the history of the Marathas, from which he has produced an interesting study of the Maratha Military System with all that it involved. Unlike one or two recent writers on the Maratha confederacy, he has avoided the temptation to twist historical facts into a basis for a political theory and his criticisms of the weak points of Maratha statecraft and organisation are on the whole fairly stated in accordance with the evidence adduced.

The Bombay Chronicle, (*Sunday, March 3, 1929*: Prof. Sen is a devoted student of Maratha History. His translations of Bakhars and of foreign biographies of Shivaji from French and Portuguese sources are well-known. His book on the Administrative System of the Marathas is a well-balanced and well-documented one. He has enhanced his reputation by the publication of this new book on the Military System of the Marathas. He has used most of the available material in all the languages and given us a good account of Maratha strength and weakness as a military power. He comes to the true conclusion that the fall of the Maratha power was due largely to its inferiority in discipline, equipment and command. The superior discipline of the early Marathas was impaired later on under the feudal revival. Their early successes were later on succeeded by defeats due to the decay of that discipline. The feudal and unorganised character of the post-Shivaji Maratha army led to its defeat and the downfall of the Maratha power. The national conception of a State and a standing army never developed after Shivaji. All the feudal elements of separatism, want of centralisation and unification remained intact.

* * * *

Prof. Sen's book is a valuable study of an important subject.

SIVA CHHATRAPATI.

Prof. Ramsay Muir: Your work bears all the marks of exact and scientific scholarship and both you and the University of Calcutta have every reason to be proud of the admirable beginning thus made in the rendering of an essential service to historical scholarship.

H. Beveridge: Mr. Sen has done good service by making a new translation of Krishnaji Sabhasad's chronicle.

C. A. Kincaid: I had myself thought of translating Sabhasad's Bakhar. But I am very glad you have saved me the trouble.

G. S. Sardesai: I have compared the translation with the original and am glad to say that it is faithful, elegant and yet quite simple.

K. N. Sane (Vivida Jnan Vistar): On the whole the work of translation has been well done.

C. H. Keith Jopp: The notes seem scholarly and the references to history all conceived in a judicial spirit.

R. N. Leslie Moore: The perusal of your work has afforded me great pleasure.

The Indian Daily News *(September, 28th, 1920)*: It is a capital book for history students.

The Englishman *(August 12th, 1920)*: Its interest and speciality consist in the author's scrupulous care to treat all available materials in an impartial and scientifically critical style.

The Bombay Chronicle *(August 30th, 1920, Dak edition)*: It speaks volumes for the ability and earnestness of Bengali scholars and for the enterprise and patriotism of the Calcutta University.

The Times of India *(26th October, 1921)*: Professor Sen and University of Calcutta have laid all students of Maratha History under a great obligation by publishing this new English edition of Krishnaji Anant's book.

The Times Literary Supplement *(23rd September. 1920)*: The life of Shivaji has been related in many chronicles, by far the most important is the contemporary chronicle by Sabhasad. A translation of this occupies pp. 1-154. It is followed by extracts from the only two other biographers whom the students are likely to consult. There are explanatory and critical notes at the end.

FOREIGN BIOGRAPHIES OF SHIVAJI.

Professor H. Dodwell: * * * * I enjoyed reading it much. The extract from Martin's Memoire seemed to me the most interesting and important, but the whole was well worth issuing. I quite agree with your very sound line of argument about Shivaji's alleged pillage and torture at Surat.

Sir Wolseley Haig: It is a most valuable contribution to the other side of Shivaji's history.

The Times Literary Supplement, *May 15th, 1930*:

In this volume Dr. S. N. Sen, who has already published two excellent studies in Maratha history, has gathered together a number of contemporary European narratives relating to Sivaji. They form a diverse and amusing collection, containing, as the editor observes, " interesting anecdote, contemporary gossip, and incidentally some information of real historical value." They include a long extract from Valentijn and other Dutch writers; from the French, the narratives of Thevenot and Carré ; and accounts of the English embassies to Sivaji. But the most interesting is undoubtedly a series of extracts from François Martin's " Memoires " which still await publication as a whole.

These provide by far the best contemporary account of Sivaji's endeavour to establish his power in Southern India in 1677. To this the French paid particular attention because of their very exposed and insecure situation, being masters, not of well-fortified and reasonably garrisoned towns like the Dutch and the English on the Coromandel coast, but of a mere indefensible and newly founded factory. Martin's sympathies lay altogether with the local Muslim ruler, Sher Khan, to whom besides the French had advanced a considerable sum of money. He visited the Khan personally, advising him to avoid a pitched battle in view of the great superiority of the Maratha forces, but to garrison and victual his chief fortresses and himself to retire to the jungles till Sivaji should be obliged by circumstances to return to his northern possessions. This sound advice was not followed. Sher Khan trusted in his Brahman astrologers, who promised him victory. He therefore advanced to meet the Marathas, but, losing his courage on a nearer view of them, he tried to break off the action, with the natural result of the complete destruction of his army. He himself took shelter in the jungles of Ariyalur, which still remained throughout the next century an impenetrable place of refuge. After this the Marathas speedily occupied all the open country ; but it is curious to find that, alert as they were, they were no betterable to prevent the Kallars—the famous thief caste —from stealing their best horses than were Clive and Lawrence in the following century. Martin records a number of instructive details regarding the administration of the conquered country. The first thing the Marathas sought was to hunt down every one who could be expected to possess any money. Then came a general resumption of grants ; even Brahman charities were not spared ; and after a brief experience of Maratha rule a number of the chief ryots took to the jungles rather than cultivate the land under the heavy terms imposed upon them. The officials, Maratha Brahman, are described as insolent and rapacious; and despite their community of caste and religion they treated Brahman and cultivators alike as conquered foreigners.

The other narrative to which we would draw special attention is the curious account by the 'Portuguese da Gurada' written in the seventeenth century. The narrative is often fantastic. It repeats the Portuguese fable that Sivaji was the son of the Portuguese lord of the village in which he was mistakenly said to have been born. It tells us that Sivaji only escaped execution at Delhi by the chance that the silver charger on which his head was to have been presented to Aurangzib was not ready in time. The writer dismisses Sivaji at his death to eternal fire, much in the spirit of the famous chronogram, " The infidel went to hell." But he gives a most picturesque account of the manner of the Moghul marches and encampments and of the Maratha methods of warfare ; and he gives characteristic detail of Sivaji himself, not only personally superintending the search after buried treasure, but also vigilantly watchful that his ministers neither oppressed his people nor defrauded his soldiers of their pay.

Statesman (*March 23, 1930*): Dr. Sen is one of the foremost authorities on Sivaji and the early history of the Marathas. He has examined more original documents connected with that portion of Maratha History which impinges on the European settlements in Western India than any other historian, and there is no one, on this side of India at least, qualified to speak with the same authority of " the last indigenous Empire-builders of India." In previous studies, Dr. Sen placed before us a careful scrutiny of the administrative and military system respectively of the Marathas. He now gives a picture of the great Sivaji seen through the spectacles of those Europeans who were either his contemporaries, or resident in India at no great space of time after his death and in doing so he includes the publication for the first time of Cosme da Guarda's Vida e Accoens do famoso felicissimo Sevagy, a rare Portuguese work which Dr. Sen copied in Lisbon, of which " only one copy found its way to India." For this reason alone the book would be a notable addition to the general literature on Sivaji, but Dr. Sen has also included an admirable translation of Barthelemy Carré's " History of Sevagy " of which only an inaccurate rendering has hitherto been available for the average Indian student. The English and Dutch records have also been laid under contribution, and the great Maratha's personality is thus most effectively and authoritatively delineated. The English accounts are drawn from unpublished papers in the India Office which Dr. Sen examined when in Europe, including accounts written by the agents of the famous Governor Aungier, one Thomas Niccolls and by Henry Oxenden. Both the Englishmen were treated with a friendly courtesy and Oxenden saw Sivaji weighed, after the old Hindu custom, against specie for charitable distribution; he weighed 1600 gold pagodas; but the most interesting account of all the European records here examined is that of the Portuguese da Guarda, who gives a detailed account of Sivaji's actual death and obsequies, and tells how the dying Sivaji gave minute instructions for certain ceremonials to be observed.... " When my soul is separated from my body, wash the body thrice in rose water of Persia which you will find in abundance in several big jars that I took from a large Persian vessel..." He also enjoined that all his wives should attend his cremation but that none of them should be forcibly burned with him...." only this courtesy from those who love me most... " Thus in full possession of his faculties died the great Maratha who was to his countrymen what Robert Bruce was to Scotland. Dr. Sen's industry and literary ability has given to many readers a picture of Sivaji that was not hitherto obtainable.

The book has valuable notes where necessary and an introduction that might have been more extensive. In it Dr. Sen satisfactorily defends Sivaji from the charge of cruelty brought against him by Sir Jadunath Sarkar who relied on the unsupported evidence of Antony Smith. Dr. Sen's more extensive researches have produced good evidence for refusing to accept Smith's allegations.

The printing is good, but some needless printer's slips have been allowed to pass ; there is an efficient index, but a map would have been a useful addition to the reader's comfort. The price of the book is not stated on the " Jacket."

It is to be hoped that Dr. Sen will bring out a complete edition of his studies of Maratha History, in a series of uniform volumes. His reputation as a scholar fully justifies such an edition for which there should be a ready demand from inside and outside India.

A PRELIMINARY REPORT ON THE HISTORICAL RECORDS AT GOA.

Principal H. G. Rawlinson: It marks a real advance in our knowledge, and I hope it will lead other workers to take up the torch.

Prof. Edgar Prestage: It will be useful to all students of Indian history of the period with which it deals.

Jules Bloch (*Journal Asiatique*): Une mission de l'Université de Calcutta a permis à M. S. Sen de faire quelques sondages dans les archives de Goa et son rapport montre par quelques exemples les ressources que les historiens de l'Inde peuvent espérer y trouver. Comme on peut s'y attendre, la plupart des documents ont trait à la politique navale des Portugais. On voit par quels moyens ils conservaient et imposaient leur souveraineté sur l'Océan ; en particulier M. Sen donne plusieurs spécimens de traités réglant avec les puissances indiennes (parmi lesquelles en 1559 le raja d'un port du Bengal) le nombre annuel, le trajet, l'armement et l'activit commerciel des bateaux autorisés à circuler. La tradition portugaise est reprise plus tard par les célèbres " pirates " Angria, puis à la fin du XVIIIe siècle par la flotte marathe.

Sur un autre point, et de facon inattendue, l'empire marathe apparaît comme un héritier : les Portugais payaient au raja de Ramnagar, le *rei choutia*, un tribut annuel dénommé *chouto* : Sivaji, qui n'éait pas né à ce moment, n'a donc pas inventé le *chauth* comme on le croyait jusqu'ici.

SOME HISTORICAL PUBLICATIONS OF THE CALCUTTA UNIVERSITY.

A History of Islamic People, by S. Khuda Bukhsh, M.A., B.C.L., Bar.-at-Law. Demy 8vo. pp. 178. Rs. 5-10.

Translated from the German of Dr. Weil's *Geschichte der islamitischen volker*—a descriptive account of Mohammad and the Quara'n as also of the Caliphate.

The Orient under the Caliphs, by the same author. Translated from Von Kremer's *Kulturgeschichte des orients*. Demy 8vo. pp. 470. Rs. 8-6.

Islamic Civilisation, Vol. I, by the same author. Demy 8vo. pp. 364. Rs. 5-0.

Do. Vol. II. Demy 8vo. pp. 309. Rs. 4-0.

The Early Heroes of Islam, by S. A. Salik, B.A. Demy 8vo. pp. 514. Rs. 6-0.

The Arab Kingdom and its Fall, by J. Wellhausen. translated into English by Margaret Graham Weir, M.A. Demy 8vo. pp. 607. Rs. 7-8.

Lectures on Arabic Historians, by Prof. D. S. Margoliouth, D.Litt., F.B.A. Demy 8vo. pp. 160+8. Rs. 2-0.

To be had of all leading book-sellers of Calcutta, Bombay and Madras.

Published by

Facsimile Publisher
Ashok Vihar, Delhi-110052 (India)
Website: www.facsimilepublisher.com

Distributed by

Gyan Books Pvt. Ltd.
5, Ansari Road, Daryaganj, New Delhi-110002 (India)
E-mail: books@gyanbooks.com, Website: www.gyanbooks.com

8 888000 549635